Rc

Thanks for purch.

Anniversary edition of the Can I Just Start Over?! book.

To express our gratitude, my team and I have developed a

bonus video with some Mindset Development tips that

we've taught leaders from across the globe. Enjoy and

keep being great!

SCAN FOR BONUS VIDEO

Can I Just Start Over?!

Printed in the United States of America

Cover Design: *Eric Bivens*

Cover Photography: *Brandon Warren*

Rousawn M. Dozier

Can I Just Start Over?!

Leveraging Lessons From Past Hardships to Design Your

Ideal Future

Rousawn M. Dozier

Dedication

Michelle - *You are my rock and greatest motivation. You're the inspiration and driving force behind this book.*

Alayah, Abrie and *Ari* - *may my ceiling in life be your floor. The responsibility of being your dad is the greatest gift I've ever been given.*

Mom and *Dad* - *You're both larger than life in your own way. I'm grateful for your love and countless lessons.*

Rousawn M. Dozier

Contents

Can I Just Start Over?!

Prologue

Victim or Victor

Have you ever asked, "*Can I just start over?*" You

know those moments in life when your back's against

the wall or when life punches you in the gut so hard

that subliminally you find yourself gasping for air? In

those moments when you want to throw in the towel

or press pause, you may wonder, "Would it be better if

I could just go back and start over and do this thing

called life all over again? Can I just start over?" The

truth is starting over is not always the best thing to do.

Rather, the most powerful thing you can do is start

fresh today by moving forward with the information

and lessons you have learned.

A couple of years ago, I heard a story that shifted my perspective. It was a story about a couple of twin boys, around the age of two or three, who had an alcoholic father. He wasn't the type of alcoholic that would have one too many, then pass out on the living room couch. No, he was a raging alcoholic, the type that would drink and come home and be physically, mentally, and emotionally abusive to everyone in the house. Those in the house were the twin boys and their mother. They recalled dozens of times where their father would physically assault their mother in front of them and then proceed to beat the boys for no reason at all. This continued into their teenage years over and over again. The abuse and mental anguish festered inside them for years, until finally, when in their thirties, the twins turned to a therapist for help.

By the time they had sought out a therapist, one of the twin boys was successful. He had joined the air force, went on to college to obtain his master's degree, and started to work for a company where he excelled. Eventually, he started his own business and before he turned thirty years old, he was already a multimillionaire. He was an incredible father to a set of twin girls and an awesome husband. The other twin had turned out quite differently. He had dabbled in drugs and alcohol and had been in and out of jail as well as rehab facilities. His life had essentially spun out of control.

The therapist asked questions, questions about how the boys coped with what they experienced, questions about how they survived difficult times. The therapist asked the brother who wasn't doing very well, "How do you think you ended up this way"? His answer was simple. He said, "I watched my father every day". The therapist directed his attention to the other brother, the brother who had found some success in his life.

He asked, "How do you think you ended up this way"?

He replied, "simple, I watched my father every day."

That's the premise of this book, *Can I Just Start Over?* It's about not going back and starting over from the beginning, but it's about leveraging the lessons from past hardships to design your ideal future. You see, *you're in control.* You can make decisions today in this moment to completely change the trajectory of your life. You don't have to hit reset and go back. You can start right here, right now with everything you've been through, take those lessons and use them to create your ideal future and accomplish all the things that you want. So can you just start over? Of course you can, but you do that by starting now. Let's go.

Chapter One

Momma's Boy

My wife and I decided after having our two beautiful daughters, Alayah and Abrie, that we were done having kids. It wasn't an easy decision (well, it kinda was LOL joking). It was a decision that we thought about, prayed about, and came to the conclusion that rather than expanding our family, we were ready to go to the next chapter of our lives. We wanted to travel and do some of those things we had not done because we had such young kids. Well, God had other plans. So, we now have three beautiful kids: our daughters, and a precious son, Ari. He's been such a blessing. In addition to him being a blessing, he's been blessed with his dad's looks (insert eye roll).

Ari and I have clicked on such an intimate level. I love taking him in the mornings while his mom catches up on some much needed rest. Even though he is only about nine months, we rough house a little bit. I love it because I feel like we're forming this bond. When I look into his eyes, I see everything that he can be. I see the man that he is going to become. I see the contribution that he's going to make to the world. I see everything and I'm so proud of him already. But in our moments together, it never fails -- his mom will walk through the hallway and his eyes go from locked-in on mine to locked it on her and he completely forgets who I am. It's super disheartening. It's like he no longer wants anything to do with his father. His eyes fill with tears. Big crocodile tears begin to roll down his face and he reaches his little arms out for his mother. He leans desperately towards her as if I'm a stranger. Per usual, his mother smiles because it makes her feel good that he wants her more than anybody else in the world. But just having real talk with you here...it bothers me. Am I jealous? Maybe a little bit. But really though, I love how he lights up when he sees his mother. He feels like everything else in the world is just gone. As long as he's with her, he's fine. I remember the first time I said to my wife, "he's such a momma's boy". She paused and looked at me with complete and utter disgust. She said, "oh yeah? It takes a momma's boy to know a mama's boy. In fact, if you look in the dictionary beside the term momma's boy, everyone would see a picture of you".

My wife is right. I am the epitome of a momma's boy and I'm not even embarrassed about it. Outside of my wife and kids, there's not a lot of people I love more than my mom. She's strong, determined, and proud. I've seen her stand in the face of adversity. I've seen her walk to and from work. I've seen her have three jobs that take care of my brother and me. Although my dad was in my life (you're going to hear more about my old man a little bit later), my mom raised my brother and me by herself, for the most part. She was relentless in her pursuit to be the best mom she could be.

My mom, Ms. Laura Darlene Dozier, is beyond human to me. From the time that I can remember, I was stuck to my mother's hip. There wasn't a place that she would go then that I wouldn't follow. If she was in the kitchen, I was in the kitchen. If she went outside, I went outside. If she was in the bathroom. Yep. As a kid (just for clarification), I was there with her. I just loved being next to my mom. I loved being in her presence. I'm a momma's boy. When I look at my son with his mother, I see the same thing. She's almost mystical to him, just like my mom was to me. She could do no wrong in my eyes because she was always there...she was consistent. I saw her set an example for my brother and me. It was incredible how she was able to walk through some of the things that she did to lead us as young men. There aren't enough words in the dictionary to describe the amount of respect, appreciation, love, and admiration that I have for that woman. The man that I am today is in large part due to the woman who raised me. I could tell you countless stories about her, countless stories about how she made people feel, countless stories about how people would just speak so highly of my mother, and they still do to this day. You see, she means so much to so many.

When I think about my mother, I think about a hurricane, not in a sense of destruction, but I think about all the things that could be going on around us, around our house, around our family. And I can remember all the chaos, all the confusion, all the trials

and tribulations. But in the eye of the hurricane, like right there in the middle was peace, grace and love. And that's why I was so close to my mother. I felt that no matter what was going on, no matter what was before us or behind us, just being in her presence would make everything alright. In fact, that is what she would tell me, that everything would be alright. And just her saying so brought this overwhelming sense of peace and calmness to my life.

I would fall, or I would get hurt and she would say to me, "son, I'm here," and I would settle down, immediately. She would then make me repeat it: "Is your mama here?" she would ask. And I would say, "Yes Ma'am." As long as I knew mom was present, I was good, and that was my life with my mother--this strong, determined, proud woman who set an example for me.

#MakeMentalHealthSexy

Can I Just Start Over?!

You know what, we don't talk much about mental health enough in this country or the world for that matter. More than 284 million people worldwide experience anxiety and depression. It's almost as if we believe that if we don't acknowledge the pain, it will just go away. *People would rather smile in public while suffering in private*. This avoidance manifests as depression, addiction, and poor habits. I want to break those chains off right now. I want children to be free. I'm done with generational curses. *You need to know that you possess the power to make your past promote you to the next level of your life*. You no longer have to be a victim. I know that we've all had challenges we've dealt with. Maybe your parents were divorced. Maybe you watched your dad walk out of your life, and you haven't even talked to him since. Maybe you experienced sexual abuse. Maybe growing up, you were so bad off financially that you were bullied and made fun of for the clothes you wore.

I don't know what your story is, **but you have the power to move past your pain and design YOUR FUTURE**. You can do it! You may be thinking to yourself, "how do you know?". I've done it; I'm not saying I'm perfect. It's taken a lot of hard work, years in fact. I still struggle. I still have moments, but it's possible. You have the power. I want to give you a tool, not the kind of tools my father-in- law keeps giving me at Christmas that I have no idea what to do with. What's the difference between a Phillips head and flat head screwdriver anyway? That conversation is for another day (definitely insert eyeroll here). But really, I want to give you an actual tool to become the master of your mindset so that you can begin designing your ideal future. This tool will require you to **ACTT**. No, not like Denzel Washington. I need you to use the acronym **A.C.T.T.**

Let me walk you through what I've done over the past few years to overcome some of the trauma I've experienced. The **A** stands for '**Acknowledgement**'. Acknowledge that you've experienced some pain in your life. Look, we've all experienced it. There is no shame in it. You don't have to hide it. You don't have to feel guilty. Just acknowledge it. Get your power back. Outside of just a few conversations with my brother and me, my mother was never very open about the pain and trauma she experienced in her life. And as a result, she found different ways to deal with it: smoking, drinking and partying. Do you also find ways to deal with the pain you're trying to avoid? Take a moment to acknowledge that you've been through something and know that it's okay to say, **"I need help"**. As I write this, I've realized that there are still some things I'm fighting that call for professional help, like therapy and counseling. Just being transparent here, I will shut the entire world out and go into manic work mode. I've found this to be as dangerous of a form of escape as any.

There is nothing wrong with receiving help. It's my goal to **make mental health sexy**. The majority of people have goals and desires of getting their physical bodies in shape. They want to be physically healthy, but what good is physical health if you're mentally and emotionally sick? I want good mental hygiene practices to get the same attention that nice summer bodies get at the beach. Speaking of that, I'm a little behind schedule on getting my summer body right LOL. Acknowledge your feelings and be okay with them. You don't need to be embarrassed. You don't need to pretend and smile in public and go home and suffer in private. I've experienced some pain, but I have the power to use it to my advantage and so do you!

Freedom

My mom and I walked a lot. Not because we were particularly health conscious but rather it was because we didn't have a car. We would also hike rides as she called it into town to my grandmother's house. As it pertained to getting to where we needed to go, she was resourceful. I grew to realize that the lack of physical resources can oftentimes cultivate incredible creativity and innovation. Anyways, back to what I was saying. When I was around 3 years old, I can remember my mother taking me to a place I called "the big house." We would get a ride into town and we would walk together to this big building, and in this office I liked it because there were a lot of toys, candy and drinks. I loved going to this big office. We went once every couple of weeks. I viewed it more as our vacation, at least to me, that is what it felt like at the time.

My mom was and still is my hero. The only thing that has changed is my perspective of what a hero is. There's something that happens when you discover your hero is actually human. There are stories of people who have gone on to meet their childhood idols only to be completely turned off in that their hero was nothing like they had envisioned. As it pertains to heros, we have a choice to make when they remove the mask and cape. We can either be disappointed by their human qualities or we can choose to embrace their flaws and that in spite of them, the hero still prevails. I have chosen the latter. That building, that big office that I loved so much wasn't this magical place that I got to go to. It was a place that my mother *had* to go to. You see, that day my mother was released from probation. The big building was nothing more than a probation office. My mother had been on probation from before the time I was born.

I remember the energy shift as we were leaving the office that day. My mother was so happy, so relieved. My mom turned to me and said, "son, we're free. We can finally do the things that we want to do. Your mom is *free*". Now, being a small boy, I had no idea what she meant. All I know is I remember walking a mile or so back to my grandmother's house.

I'd be remiss not to introduce you to my grandmother. It's been said that I have a 'polarizing' personality. Though I don't believe that to be true. However, if I'm even remotely polarizing, I would have gotten that from my grandmother, Deborah Simms aka Debbie Dozier. She remains the most polarizing person I've ever met. Never one to hold her tongue, you always knew exactly where you stood with her. Some may call her approach to communication tough or even harsh. I consider it direct, cut to the chase feedback.

For as blunt as she was, there was a magnetic aura

to her. People of all ages, backgrounds and walks of

life would flock to her living room because of the

authenticity, transparency and love they felt in her

presence. Truth be told, as I'm writing this, I wish I

could spend one more afternoon with her at this point

in my life. I'm one thousand percent certain that I'd

leave the room knowing exactly where I need to get

better in my life but most importantly, I'd leave having

experienced love and connection that only she was

able to give. Oh yea, I was in the middle of a story

here.

As my mother and I entered the door, my

grandmother, who's never had a loss of words,

seemed to be anticipating what my mother was going

to say. They locked eyes with one another. And my

mom said to her mother, "I'm free. I'm done with my

probation". My grandmother, in true Debra Dozier fashion said, "Well, you know what that means. It's time to roll up now". Let me give you some context as to what 'roll up' means. It doesn't mean fruit roll-ups. It doesn't mean a pastry roll up. It means roll up some weed. What I grew accustomed to was that weed smoke was no different than cigarette smoke. For the most part, everyone in my life smoked weed. It was completely normal to me. It was part of my everyday life. What I didn't realize at the time is that my mother hadn't been able to smoke weed in years because of her probation. Well, that day is when my hero began to have human qualities, in my eyes. I remember mom sitting down and giving me my action figures to pass the time. While I was playing with them and doing things I wasn't supposed to be doing, for about two hours, my mom, my grandmother and the people that came in to celebrate this monumental moment of my mom being released from probation.

Yes, technically, my mother was 'free'. She would no longer be required to attend probation meetings or adhere to additional monitoring. However, she was still very much chained. Mentally and emotionally, she was shackled to the past. Sadly, many people are enslaved and entangled by past experiences. If these chains are not dealt with, they will keep you in bondage your entire life, resulting in things like depression, anxiety, addictions. and bad. My hero, my mother had flaws. My mother was very much enslaved and imprisoned. My hero was human. I got to see it up close and personal. Once you've **acknowledged** your pain, it's time to move to the next letter of the *ACTT* acronym.

The *C* represents '**Change**'; as in change your perspective. I vividly remember getting out of my Uber and walking into the beautiful Loews Hotel in Atlanta, GA (they're not even paying me for that name drop lol). As I was making my way into the hotel, I noticed one of the biggest trucks I had ever seen in my entire life. The tires on the truck were as tall as me. The truck itself was transporting what appeared to be boulders. I know it was just a truck but I had literally never seen a truck of that size. Upon getting checked into my room, I immediately FaceTimed my wife so that I could see her beautiful face and yes, show her the truck that I was fascinated by. As I looked down from the top floor, I couldn't immediately find the truck. I could make out what appeared to be the same truck that I had seen just moments before but it looked significantly smaller. I literally said to my wife, "that thing was massive when I was on the same level as it".

That's what happens when you *change* your perspective about things that you've gone through in life. Things that were once massive become seemingly smaller. I'm not saying that what you've gone through is small or insignificant, but as you change your perspective, you begin seeing the larger picture. You don't have to let your experiences define you. Take your power back by changing your perspective. The pain is actually preparing you for what you're called to do. That divorce doesn't define you nor is it a giant in your life. The financial hardship you've experienced hasn't paralyzed you. The addiction you suffered through will not hinder you. God called and created you in His image. *Take your power back by changing your perspective!*

It's Complicated

My mom's background was super complicated. She suffered so many trials and tribulations and faced many hardships and losses. At times my mom would share stories with my brother and me about the struggles of my grandmother. Like so many people in the 1970's and 1980's, my grandmother fell victim to the drug epidemic that ravaged the country. Truth be told, there wasn't much support in the lower income communities for people who were addicted. In those times, the addicts weren't labeled as 'sick'. They would either use drugs until they died or be thrown into jail -- leaving their children to fend for themselves or be taken away by Child Protective Services (CPS).

There's one story in particular that I remember my mother telling. She was around the age of 9 and she and her siblings were in the apartment alone and had been for a number of days. Desperate to not alarm anyone that they were home alone and also to feed my uncle who was not much older than 1 year old; she opened a can of corn and proceeded to feed him and her siblings. Tears would run down her face as she'd share that story as well as similar ones with my brother and me.

Her sacrificial spirit carried over as she raised my brother and me. She sacrificed on a daily basis. She sacrificed her needs, her desires to make sure we had what we needed. Given her childhood and the circumstances in which she was raised, the fact that she would love us enough to sacrifice herself for us is something that I'll never truly be able to thank her enough for. But these types of circumstances, these types of experiences, if not dealt with, can place chains on your mind and heart.

When my mother was around 10 years old, my grandmother was convicted of murder, which my family now knows was self- defense (which was proven in court). Nonetheless, CPS took my mother and her siblings into the 'system'. My mom went to live with her aunt who already had ten kids of her own. In total, there were fifteen people living in a three-bedroom house. Sometimes, there was not enough food to eat, so my mom and her cousins would often sneak over into an orchard that was adjacent to the house and pick peaches from the tree. One day, the owner of the orchard came outside and began shooting in the kids' direction with a high-powered BB gun, and it struck my mom several times. Even as an adult there were still several pellets in her skin that were never taken care of. That's how mental health begins to deteriorate, things that are supposed to come out stay bottled up. At the age of 12, my mom picked up the habit of smoking cigarettes, not because she liked cigarettes, but because smoking cigarettes in the outhouse kept the bugs away. She hated going to the outhouse. In fact, she was disgusted by it and felt it was beneath her, so for weeks and months she didn't use the bathroom. As a result, her stool backed up in her intestines. One day at school she passed out and had to be rushed to the emergency room to undergo surgery.

She almost died because there was something on the inside of her that needed to pass, but she wouldn't pass it because of where she was. I think about my mom's story now, and it is a reminder that if we allow what hurts us to build up on the inside of us; if we do not treat the hurt and let it pass, we can die. Maybe it won't be a physical death but rather a psychological death, which depending upon who you ask could be worse. Truth is, you can live your entire life as if you're dead, without true joy, happiness, vision or hope for better days. As you read this, please take inventory of the chains that have wrapped themselves around your mind and emotions. I'll say it again, take your power back by changing your perspective! I know, I know. You're probably thinking, "how do I change my perspective"? Thanks for asking (lol), that brings us to the next letter, of **ACTT**, *T*.

The first *T* is for **'Tactical'**. This part is so vital for long term success. You need to determine healthy and *tactical* practices to keep the chains off of your mind. Ask yourself this, what will take the pain's place? The same energy you've spent focusing on what was hurting you needs to be harnessed to something that's productive, lifegiving and serves you. I don't know exactly what this will look like for you but for me, it meant being intentional in my mind, body, relationships and resources. It's still a work in progress but I've been able to craft a set of tactical steps that I can measure on a weekly basis.

I use a tactical approach that I refer to as **D3**: *Decision, Direction and Discipline*. Make a decision on where you want to go from where you're currently at. I encourage you to literally sit down and make the decision in more than just one area. Determine where you want to be 12 months from now in your mind, body, relationships and resources. Once you've done that, begin putting together a road map of steps it will take to get to the destination. This is what I refer to as directions. Don't skip this part of the tactical process. The directions will keep you from veering off and getting lost on the journey. The final component to D3 is discipline. If you're truly going to get to the next level in your life, it's going to require discipline. Yup, *doing what you said you were going to do long after the feeling you had when you said it is gone.* Remember, **a new level of you is going to require a new version of you**.

Can I Just Start Over?!

Prison or Promotion

When my mother was fifteen years old, her mother came home from prison, and she welcomed all the kids back home. They moved back into town. My mom went to high school, and it seemed like she was finally free, free to be a kid, free to go to school...free to live. Still, there was undealt with pain on the inside of her. She would often wish and dream of being in a house with parents that loved her, having things of her own, being able to be a cheerleader, which is one of the things she always said she wanted to do. To this day, I can't help but to feel bad. These are things that many people take for granted, myself included.

Shortly after returning home with my grandmother, my mom began using and selling drugs. You see in the 80s, the crack epidemic broke out and people all around the city had fallen victim to addiction. My mom

sold enough so that she could continue to use it.

Eventually, she began dating one of the biggest drug

dealers in the area. A few years into her hustle, she

got busted and went to jail. The cops came into the

house and arrested my grandmother, again. My

grandmother then took the cops to where my mother

was. They cuffed my mother and brought her out. As

they put my mother in the cop car next to her mother,

my aunt Krissy who was around 16 at the time chased

the cop car down the road, completely distraught.

Both her mother and oldest sister being stripped of

their freedom right in front of her.

My mom got arrested just a little bit before I was

conceived. Instead of being imprisoned, she was

placed on probation. Yes, the same probation that she

would be freed from the day I referred to her as my

hero, but with the physical shackles and chains gone,

she began smoking weed, and it's something she'd do throughout my entire life. The demons, the internal struggles, and invisible forces would rear their ugly heads and instead of dealing with the past, she tried to run from it. She'd go out and party and drink and do things she knew she was better than, but she couldn't stop because she never dealt with the demons. That's my challenge to you. Please take the time to deal with the internal demons and struggles. I'm just a *momma's boy* who wants to let you know that **your past can be your prison or your promotion**. If you're reading this right now, you possess the power to take hold of your past. It does not have to be your prison. You do not have to be restricted by invisible chains that are wrapping around your mind and derailing your future. You have the power to design your destiny. You just need to use and leverage the lessons you've experienced.

Now that you've learned how to **acknowledge** the pain of your past; take back the power by **changing** your perspective and utilizing **tactical** tools, it's time for the final and most important component of the ACTT acronym.

The final *T* stands for **'Teach'**. It's time to *teach* someone else how you faced your past and used your experiences to propel you forward. ***With every opportunity comes responsibility***. If you're reading this, you've been gifted the opportunity to be alive, so with that comes responsibility. It's my belief that teaching and helping others is the reason for our existence. If you're anything like me, you may feel like you aren't qualified, capable or worthy enough to teach anyone how to do anything. I promise you are. In fact, it's imperative that you use your experiences to show people that they too can overcome obstacles and adversity.

That's what we're going to do. We're going to take action. That's what this book is all about. It's about looking your past in the face and identifying lessons you learned along the way. It's about overcoming adversity. It's about recognizing that there's a power deep down on the inside that needs to come out, because the world needs what you have. *The past can be your prison, or it can be your promotion* and in this book, I want you to know that it's promotion time. It's time to go to that next level, then the level after that. It's time to live a life so big that you're going to say, "I never thought this was possible." Truth is, you don't need to go back and start over. You just need to start over by starting right here, right now with everything you've learned. My prayer is that you learn a lot more about yourself through the reading of this book. Thank you for journeying with me, let's go!

Chapter Two

Laundry

"Ew, something stinks," said my third-grade classmate, my crush as I walked by her after sharpening a No. 2 pencil. I sat directly behind her. I liked her from the very first day of class. I remember looking at her hair and being interested in what she was going to wear. I would imagine what we had in common. And the very first thing she said to me, was, "something stinks". Every five minutes she'd turn around and ask me if I smelled cheese puffs. She just didn't know where it was coming from. And, of course, in shrewd Rousawn Dozier fashion, I made a joke that changed the subject. I was a deflector; it started early

in my life. To this day, I either deflect or bulldoze when things get tense or the atmosphere changes.

For the rest of the day, I found myself avoiding classmates. Instead of playing basketball, I sat back and just hung out. Even following recess, I made the slow journey down the hall, turned left past the cafeteria, and walked into my elementary classroom. I remember like it was yesterday because I told my teacher that I wasn't feeling well. I was lying, but I just wanted to get out of the classroom, get to the nurse's office and sit there. Why? I knew my mother wasn't going to come pick me up. We didn't have a car.

I knew my mom didn't know anyone that could come pick me up. In fact, I knew that my mom was working. I just wanted to be out of the classroom. I wanted to be away from my peers. I didn't want to be the subject of any jokes because other classmates had accused others of smelling like an old baseball mitt or like old socks. The truth is as embarrassed as I was, I knew it was me in that moment. I knew the socks and underwear I was wearing had been worn more than once. In fact, they hadn't been washed between the last two times that I wore them.

So yeah, I was a little insecure. I was moving slowly because I knew I smelled badly, but more importantly, the emotional scars of what happened to me made me feel even worse. I just wanted to go home that day. I just wanted to get on the bus, forget everything that was said, and escape all the eyes I imagined were looking at me. I was wondering if they were looking at me in judgment, knowing that I was the person that smelled bad. Finally, the end of the day came and the bus arrived. I walked all the way to the back and sat down by myself.

I gazed out the window as the bus passed doctors' offices, different housing developments, and I thought

to myself, *What would it be like to live in a house?*
What would it be like to have a car? What would it be
like to be able to go places when we wanted to go
and not have to rely on someone to take us out? I
thought to myself, *What would it be like to even step*
foot in a house? Up until that point, I had never been
in a house. We lived in one of the larger low-income
apartment complexes in the city, Martinsburg, West
Virginia. I didn't even know anyone that owned a
house. I barely knew anyone that owned a car. As my
head rested against the window, I closed my eyes,
trying to envision how awesome it would be to have a
car. As soon as the picture was clear in my mind, the
bus stopped. We were back home, at my stop.

It was time to get off the bus and go home and take
care of all the things I needed to handle. But I wasn't
alone, I had my brother with me. My brother was in
first grade at the time, and it was my job to make sure

we made it from the bus stop back to our apartment. We had to walk through some of the harshest conditions in my city at that time.

Finally, we made it to the apartment. I took the key out of my backpack and put it into the handle, turned it and pushed. It was a huge heavy metal door. It almost took both of us to get into the apartment. When we got inside, I grabbed a stool, stood up and chained the door at the top (per my mother's orders). This is what we did every single day. As my brother went to throw his book bag down on the couch, I grabbed the note my mom left:

I love you both. For dinner tonight, boil a few hot dogs. There's a couple left. We don't have buns, so just use a piece of bread. Also, make sure all homework is done and be sure you get in bed before 9:00 PM. Lastly, I left $4 in quarters. Try to come up with another dollar to dry clothes for the laundry.

- *Love, Mom.*

That year, we would walk into an empty apartment on a pretty regular basis, it wasn't an unusual occurrence. My mom worked from 8:00 in the morning until 5:00 in the afternoon, so there was no way that she could have picked us up after school. We didn't exactly have the money for a babysitter, so it was my responsibility to make sure everything was handled until my mom got home.

Most days, my mom wouldn't get home usually until bedtime because after leaving the job that she worked at through the day, she'd go to Sheetz, where she had picked up a job in the evenings. There was something in the letter that bothered me. It wasn't the fact that we were having hotdogs for what felt like the tenth time in ten days. It wasn't the fact that we were out of buns. It was the fact that I had to somehow come up with a couple of dollars in quarters. That's not that big of a deal, except I knew I'd have to ask a couple of our neighbors. I absolutely hated asking people for stuff. Even at a young age, I just hated asking for things, even if it was something I really needed, like a dollar to be able to do a load of laundry.

Asking for help is still something I struggle with today. I don't know why I struggle with that. I can recall times, even recently when I actually needed help but was too afraid or even proud to ask. I've come to realize that I struggle with thinking that asking for help somehow equates to weakness. However, I know that's not true. In fact, it's the opposite of weak. Knowing when to ask, who to ask and how to ask for help is a sign of strength. With that being said, I'm still working on getting better at asking for help.

As I stood in the kitchen reading the note my mom left, there was another reason I didn't want to ask for quarters. I was cognizant of the fact that people who lived where we lived just didn't have it. I lived in what's called section 8 housing. Essentially, it's low-income housing for individuals and families who can't afford a mortgage or can't afford a nicer apartment. It's for people who are literally going through some difficult seasons. It's for people who are fighting to survive. So no, people didn't have stuff, and that's why it was so hard for me to ask for something that seemed as trivial as $2 dollars in quarters. However, I knew the clothes had to be washed. I may have been wearing the same underwear to school the next day and there was no way I was going to let that happen.

I sat down and I began to think, "how can I get a couple of dollars"? *Make a phone call.* I would have loved to have made a phone call, but the reality was we didn't have a phone yet. Not only that, but no one in my building had a phone with the exception of one of my mom's friends. My building had eight different apartment units. Each one had two bedrooms. Space was tight. Only a handful of people had vehicles of their own. Even food and clothes were scarice.

I looked up, and I saw my Nerf water gun. It was one of my favorite things to play with. There was a kid, Timmy who lived in the unit directly beneath ours - he was about a grade younger than I was, and he constantly wanted to borrow the water gun but I wasn't allowed to lend it to him. An idea jumped into my head, I could lend it to him for a dollar a day. Even at a young age, I had an entrepreneurial spirit. I realized that if I could provide or exchange value, I could generate money.

Being raised in an environment of scarcity meant that money was seen as a solution to problems. As I mentioned, it wasn't just my family that struggled, it was just about every person who lived in my apartment complex. Know this, when your mind is constantly in lack or survival, it's difficult to think abundantly. So yes, we felt like we had 'money problems', when in fact, we had mindset problems. Some of the most incredible people I know, I met growing up in the projects. I met some of the most resourceful and creative thinkers. Sadly, a few of them ended up in prison or even dead. Why am I sharing this? I want you to ask yourself if the perceived problems you have are *circumstantial problems* or *mindset problems*. Is your marriage a problem or is it your mindset? Is your money a problem or is it your mindset? ***I believe with every fiber of my DNA that your mindset will either set you up in life or set you back in life***. You get to decide if you want to master your mind or remain slave to it.

As I made my way down the stairs towards Timmy's apartment, I was conflicted. I didn't want to part with my water gun because I loved it. But, I was also afraid that my mother would be mad because she specifically told me to never lend it out to people. Regardless, I was willing to deal with the repercussions of her wrath to keep me from asking around for change.

Knock, knock, knock.

"Hey Timmy", I said as his little body opened the door.

"Hey, Sean (yes people called me and still do call me Sean). What are you doing here?", said Timmy.

"I have something for you", I said.

Timmy's eye's shot directly to the water gun. He was so excited.

"Are you giving it to me?" he exclaimed.

"Kinda. I'm not actually giving it to you. I'm gonna let you borrow it". "Thank you." said Timmy.

Can I Just Start Over?!

"Well, I'm going to let you borrow it, but I need money", I said.

"Money? How much money", Timmy asked.

Tim lived with his mom and for whatever reason, she would give him her leftover change at the end of each week. He would put the change into a big dingy sock. I saw this sock during multiple ice cream truck runs. That and/or food stamps (can you believe the ice cream truck took food stamps? I believe we called it the crab truck, such good times).

I said, "Timmy, I'm going to let you use the water gun for two days. I just need you to get me eight quarters."

Timmy slowly closed the door and returned just moments later with his dingy coin filled sock. He proceeded to pull out eight quarters and placed them in my hand.

I smiled, happy I didn't have to go around asking neighbors for quarters. The smile was short lived when I was reminded by Timmy pulling that water gun away from me that I'd be without my favorite toy for a couple of days. I went upstairs to cook dinner. Okay, not exactly to cook but to boil hotdogs, which is what we did (if you've never had boiled hotdogs, you're missing out!).

Once we finished dinner, it was about 6:00pm. I knew I needed to take the clothes downstairs and get ready to wash them. $2.00 per load to wash and $1.00 per load to dry. I wonder how many washing machines and dryers the people in my apartment building could have purchased over the years considering the amount of money spent washing clothes. It's not total exploitation but it's pretty close.

An unspoken rule when washing clothes in our building was, DO NOT LEAVE YOUR CLOTHES

Can I Just Start Over?!

UNOCCUPIED! It was nothing out of the ordinary for people's clothes to be stolen out of the washer or dryer. One of the first physical altercations I had ever seen wasn't over money necessarily. It wasn't over anything other than a few articles of clothing coming up missing from the laundry room. As you read this, it might be hard to imagine people fighting over clothes but it's a reality of a lot of people in the world today. So, there I was, sitting in the laundry room, making sure no one laid a hand on our clothes. I was willing to fight, scratch and claw to ensure our clothes made it back to our apartment. I was willing to do whatever had to be done to protect the clothes that were in that washer machine because they belonged to me. They belonged to my family.

Later that night I was eating my hot dog and doing my homework. I was thinking about what I had seen earlier that day while on the school bus. Swimming pools, people in cars, nice houses. I told myself I didn't need any of that. At that moment, I just wanted a washing machine -- a washing machine that was in our house, a washing machine that didn't need quarters, a washing machine that didn't require me to ask people for quarters.

As much as I hated to take my clothes downstairs to the laundromat to wash, it actually taught me subconsciously to fight for what was important. I learned to fight for what was mine. The dirty laundry experience taught me that if something belongs to me, you would have to kill me to take it. What does that look like now?

At the time I'm writing this book, I have my own washer and dryer, a backyard, a house and cars and all the things that I wanted when I was a kid, but it's not those things that make me happy. That's what I learned as I listened to my clothes being washed. It wasn't all my stuff, but it was what it meant to me. It was the dream that I had down in my heart to make something of myself. It was the desire to want more for people, to be able to serve and help. Now, it's the relationship with my wife and kids. You will never take that from me without killing me first because I learned that if it's mine, I will *fight for it.*

What are you fighting for? As you're reading these pages, perhaps my story is similar to yours. Maybe it's not close to what you experienced but that doesn't matter. The question remains, what are you fighting for? Are you willing to fight for that relationship? Are you willing to fight for your place in this world? Are you willing not to let a man or woman keep you from what God has called you to?

Truth is, I've seen a lot of people just give up. *I've seen a lot of people fall victim to their past, allowing the pain to paralyze them of their tomorrow.* I've seen people not take a risk or bet on themselves. I've seen people choose not to fight, but completely give up. I don't want that for you. This book is my heart. It's my life, but it's a manifesto that says, if you just fight, you can have whatever it is that you desire, you're both worthy and deserving of it. I know the divorce may have hurt. I know the lack of having a mom or dad in your life left scars. Are you willing to fight for the life you deserve despite what you've experienced in the life you've lived thus far? Maybe your back is on the canvas of life at this point. I not only encourage you to forget about giving up. I'm encouraging you to get up, put your chin up and upper-cut whatever is keeping you from becoming the best version of you.

Chapter Three

Vacation

"Here, put this in a bag, boy" says my mom. My brother, mom and myself were packing for our first ever trip to the beach. We had talked about this moment for such a long time. We were beyond excited that the time had finally come. We talked about swimming in a hotel swimming pool and how great the experience would be. Here's the thing, neither one of us could swim at the time, but we were still so excited for the opportunity to go to the beach.

I mean, up until that point and my nine years on earth, I only traveled about fifteen to twenty minutes outside of my hometown. I'd been to Hagerstown, Maryland. It only took fifteen minutes to get there. Winchester.

Virginia, another fifteen minute trip. My world felt big
at the time but knowing what I know now, my
experiences were extremely limited. The closest thing
to a vacation I'd ever been on was a school field trip
to Harpers Ferry, West Virginia, about twenty miles
away from my elementary school. It felt like I was a
world away. I had never been that far out. We rode
through the mountains, from county to county, seeing
the landscape change, seeing shops I'd never seen. I
may as well have been on the other side of the
country. I remember walking through the historic
Harpers Ferry, rich in Civil War history that saw
countless battles in which the North was fighting to
liberate my people from slavery. We heard many
awesome stories, but vividly I remember the armory.
We walked into the very same armory that John
Brown, the famous American abolitionist, had an
expectation to overtake. He used the weapons to

equip slaves and abolitionists to fight the Confederate army. The tour guide showed us where John Brown would have rallied the troops, where he would have given incredible speeches to empower people to be their best selves, where he would have painted a picture that was so much bigger than any one particular person. He was willing to sacrifice everything to free people from bondage.

It was the first time I'd ever heard about him. Brown's story inspired me to want to have a major impact on people. I wanted one day to do something that was much bigger than myself. I wanted to help free people. It was a long-shot, given the fact that I'd never even been out of my hometown, given the fact that I'd never even experienced life, but something that day clicked in me. I wanted to create something or be a part of a movement that freed people, I just couldn't see it yet. However, a few things I learned along the way:

One - never judge someone just because they don't do what it is you think they should do. *Two* - never judge a person's intellect or their heart. Sometimes opportunities are different for people. Sometimes people feel they have to take care of themselves and their family and there's only one way to do it.

As I sat on the edge of the bed in the bottom bunk trying to figure out which of my twelve Batman action figures I wanted to take to the beach, I had a different type of expectation. I didn't have the expectation of freeing people that had been enslaved in chains for hundreds of years. I didn't have an expectation to lead a revolt to risk my life. At that moment, my expectation was for someone to come and loosen the chains off my reality and allow my family and me to experience something we'd never experienced, but it wasn't going to be John Brown coming to liberate me. It was going to be my stepdad. I absolutely loved my stepdad, Dwight. In fact, I still do. He was one of the only men I knew in addition to my father (we'll talk about him later) but Dwight was the other male influence in my life. He was younger than my dad and cooler too. Not only did my brother and I love him, my friends loved him, too. He'd take us places around town and get us ice cream. He played basketball with us, and he was so much different than the other guys in the neighborhood.

Dwight grew up in Philadelphia, Pennsylvania. His life was different. He was exposed to things that even I wasn't exposed to. He was exposed to unprecedented violence. He was exposed to crime. He was exposed to the drug trade and as charming and charismatic as he was, there was another side of him that I wouldn't see until so many years later, but he taught me so

much. Some good, some bad. He taught me more through his actions than he could ever have taught me through his words. For so long, I wanted to be just like him. Even to this day, there's a part of me that does resemble him in certain ways, especially as it relates to entrepreneurship and business.

Back to the beach. I grabbed my toys and threw them into our shared suitcase, it almost felt like the night before Christmas! Like when you can barely rest and you're hanging with your siblings, anticipating the toys that are going to be under the tree and when you spend the next day going around the neighborhood sharing with all your friends. That's the type of energy my brother and I had. I was in bed at 7:30pm trying to force myself to go to sleep because I was already envisioning the wind hitting my face and the sand between my toes. I could hear the laughter. I could feel it.

Can I Just Start Over?!

We finally fell asleep after tossing and turning and after my mom threatened to spank our butts. We woke up at 5:00 a.m. the next morning. We were so excited. We didn't need breakfast. We brushed our teeth, put our clothes on and anxiously waited for Dwight to pick us up; it was going to be awesome. We sat on the couch and watched cartoons to pass time. Mom was cooking breakfast with a smile on her face due to my brother and I's excitement. She showed us pictures of what our hotel room was going to look like as well as the view from the balcony.

In our minds, we were already there, but the clock was dragging. I could almost hear the ticks like someone was shooting a gun beside me. Minutes seemed like hours; hours seemed like months and though we woke up at five o'clock, it was only 7:10am. We still had two hours before Dwight would be there to pick us up. In an effort to pass time and burn off some energy, mom sent us outside to play along with the instructions to NOT get our clothes dirty. Around nine o'clock my mom came outside to summon us in to get cleaned up before we got on the road. I had never run so hard in my life. I was simply a kid that wanted to be outside, but not on that day -- I wanted to get in the house and get ready to go on vacation.

9:00am came, I was looking out the window. I walked over to the balcony looking at the road that led into our apartment complex. Nine-thirty came, but there was still no Dwight. Being late was not completely out of character for him. Dwight was always hustling and bustling; moving and shaking. He was always about an hour late. When 10:00am came around, I knew something was different. No one had sent any message that he wasn't coming. And I say no one sent any message because we didn't have a phone.

Mom walked across the street to her friend's house to use the phone.

She came back fifteen minutes later. My brother asked if she had spoken to Dwight and if he was on his way. She said she couldn't reach him. Another hour came and went. I started to get nervous. I was thinking about the beach, the experience of just getting out of town and I began to feel it was not going to happen. At 11:30am, my mom walked back across the street to use the phone. Silence filled the room as my brother and I waited on my mother to come back and give us the news on Dwight's status. She returned after what seemed like an eternity. Her face was full of disappointment. Her voice broke the heavy silence that had covered the room. I can remember her saying to me, "boys, Dwight's not coming". Why did we even get our hopes up?

"How about we go over and go swimming across town?" my mother asked. On the outside, she appeared bold and confident and ready to take on the world, but something on the inside of her seemed frail, sad, and hurt. When I looked into her eyes, it almost seemed as though she knew we were being let down.

Neither my brother nor myself said anything as it related to the beach. Though we were young, we knew that how we handled the disappointment would weigh heavily on our mother. So, we unpacked our swim trunks and floaties and walked across town to Lambert pool. Lambert pool was awesome. Well, not really but it beat sitting in the apartment all day. Lambert pool did however have the best hot dogs ever. Essentially, they were boiled, then topped with nacho cheese. They cost a dollar, but sometimes I would charm the cashier with my smile, and she would give it to me for fifty cents. My brother would always buy Twizzlers. It took about thirty minutes to get to the pool on foot. I can't remember much about the conversation. I just remember seeing the determination in my mom's eyes, the fight, the resolve in her spirit, and her refusal to let my brother and me be hurt.

My brother was smiling, seemingly forgetting all about the beach trip we were supposed to be on. I couldn't help but begin to feel some resentment, not just against Dwight, but even against my mom and other adults in my life. Here I was being let down…. again. We were supposed to be in an air-conditioned car on our way to Ocean City, MD to find seashells, eat out, to be on a beach walking. Instead I'm walking across town in 90+ degree temperatures. To top it all off, I was embarrassed. I had bragged to all of my friends that we'd be leaving for the beach that day. These are the same friends I'd likely have to face at the pool. Upon arriving at Lambert Pool, my mom went up to the individual taking the money. Without giving her any cash, she turned around and told us to go ahead and go in.

What I later discovered is that my mom didn't have any money. She explained to the young lady what happened, and I guess out of pity, she felt bad for us and let us in for free. Lambert had a big open space on the side where everybody gathered, threw down towels, and laid out in the sun. Some even brought food. My mom instructed my brother and I to stay out of the deep end and sent us on our way.

I stepped down into the warm, chlorine-filled water, thinking that it was supposed to be salt water and sand. To top it all off, the pool was most certainly pee-filled as well (insert another eye roll here). As I sat down in the pool, I felt different. This stung a little more than the other times I had been let down.

Long before the days of YouTube and Instagram there was a VHS tape that was probably thirty minutes, (yes I said VHS - Video Home System) it had a virtual tour guide that would take you on a journey through every single Walt Disney World park: Magic Kingdom, Animal Kingdom, Epcot and MGM Studios, now known as Hollywood Studios. It included everything--the restaurants, the rides, the characters. You name it -- it was on the VHS. Everything but the price that is.

My brother and I would watch this tape, and we would feel like we were at Disney World. We would talk about going. It was going to be great. We told our friends at school and for months we looked forward to it, only to be let down. We ended up going to the skating rink in Hagerstown instead. I had nothing against skating. It just wasn't Disney World.

Eventually, I would have to go back and face my

friends who I told we were getting Mickey ears and

those big round suckers. They'd always laugh and

say, "told you so". I was the sucker.

I was discouraged, but never like this. This one hurt

differently because of who let me down. A man I

loved, respected, and trusted let me down. Something

shifted in me that day. Something changed. I

promised myself that I would never expect anything

from anybody ever again. That day, I determined that I

wasn't going to open up so that people could hurt me.

I didn't want to give people the real estate in my mind

or heart. I just wasn't going to expect anything from

anyone again!

No one ever came out and said that we weren't going

to the beach. But upon walking home from Lambert, a

few hours later, it was confirmed that we wouldn't be

going. Shortly after arriving back to our apartment, one of my mother's friends knocked on the door and my mother excused herself and stepped out to talk. Trying to make out what was going on, I put my ear to the door to listen, but couldn't come up with anything. A couple of minutes later, my mom came back inside and said,"Hey boys, Dwight won't be back for a while".

I was watching TV and eating stovetop popcorn. Sidebar, If you've never had stovetop popcorn, you're missing out. Well, I don't know about that. I'm still pulling kernels out of my teeth from 20 years ago (lol). Anyways, back to the story.

I glanced up at my mother with a face and stone and responded "where is he?".

"On vacation" she replied.

"On Vacation?" I asked, questioning those very words. "We were supposed to go on vacation with him". As she gazed down towards the ground and her arm resting on the doorway, my mother responded quietly but in a stern manner, "Well, he's on a different type of vacation".

"When's he coming back?" I said.

"I don't know baby, but don't worry." my mother said, softly.

She began to appear blurry as tears of sadness and disappointment filled my eyes. A lump in my throat made it nearly impossible to swallow. I wanted to shout and scream. I couldn't believe that we were being let down...again. Yet, I knew that what was happening was outside of my mother's control.

"Sean" my mother said. Trying to cut through the tense atmosphere.

"Yes ma'am." I responded.

"Is your mom here?" she said with a slight grin.

I didn't respond. I knew where she was going with this. I'd been here before. I was angry. I have an expectation for the people in my life to do what they said they were going to do and when they don't do it, I'm hurt.

"Answer me!" she demanded. "Yes, ma'am." I said.

"Then you're fine. You'll be alright as long as I'm here." my mother said.

Maybe you've been there. Maybe you were twenty-five when the walls went up. Maybe you were two or five. ***The walls we build will keep us from the destinies that are supposed to be ours***. Those walls that are built from disappointment will keep us from everything that we're supposed to have. ***When we've experienced hurt, we fortify walls instead of having fulfillment***. We live behind these barriers, trying to protect ourselves, and as a result, we don't experience the trueness and richness of life. That was me. That's what I did with the expectations. But here's the thing. *When you stop having expectations, you can't expect to live a fulfilled life.* Expectations are real.

I can remember the intense feeling of anger I had walking into school the morning after finding out that my stepdad's vacation was actually a maximum security prison. You see, what makes Dwight a person I admire is his charisma and business-savvy. The only issue was that instead of doing legitimate entrepreneurship, he dealt drugs because that is what he was exposed to as a kid. That's why he didn't come get us for the beach. That was the vacation he was on.

There were so many expectations, so many things I wanted him to see that year. I was actually getting pretty good at basketball. I wanted Dwight to see me play for the first time. I wanted him to see me play football. I carried that anger, resentment, and bitterness all the way into my classroom that morning. I sat not knowing how to articulate or deal with what I was feeling. One of my classmates, just goofing off as he always did, said a couple of things to me and poked fun at me. Without thinking, I flipped the desk in front of me. Pens, paper, pencils and textbooks went everywhere.

I realized what I did was wrong, but at that moment, I was angry. I yelled at the kid, "Leave me alone!" My teacher stood up: "Sean Dozier, go to the office!" I looked at her, tears rolling down my face, fist clenched, ready to take action against any person or anything that came my way. Heart beating rapidly and breathing heavily, I backed out of the room, gazing at each one of my classmates. The walk to the principal's office broke my heart because I realized it wasn't me that I let down. My mother was going to get a call at work, and she was going to have to find a way to get to the school to pick me up. She wasn't going to be able to go back to work because of my actions.

I began to ask myself questions: *Why didn't my teacher ask me what was wrong? Why didn't she send me to the guidance counselor instead? Why am I walking to the principal's office?* You know what, upon arriving at the principal's office, not once did she ask me what was bothering me. Not once did she ask me what was wrong. The action I took in that classroom was outside of what I typically did. Not one time did she ever ask me, "How can I help you?" She just handed me a one-day suspension, and that's the day I realized that no one cared about what I was going through. My expectations for the adults who I loved and who had responsibility for me, including teachers, changed dramatically. At an elementary age, I built psychological walls. I said, "You're not going to hurt me." Decades later, I'm just now learning how to tear down those walls I built because of the experiences I had.

As I've looked back at moments like this in my life, I've realized my biggest expectations should be for myself because I can't expect more from someone else than I expect from me. So how can we manage our expectations and allow them to work for us rather than against us? Starting now, we can leverage our expectations so that we can be effective. These are some tools that have helped me to healthily manage expectations:

- *Be open*! Not long ago, I was trying to make it all the way across town in about 9 minutes before the bank closed. Someone had recently written me a check (who writes checks these days LOL, joking -- I'll definitely take your check) and I was trying to make it do the bank to make a deposit. As soon as I made it to the bank's parking lot, I could see the teller flip the closed sign and pull down the curtain. At that moment, it didn't matter that I had something of value to deposit because the institution was closed. Are you trying to figure out where I'm going with this (LOL)? The point that I'm trying to make is, if someone has something of value to offer you, they'll never be able to make the deposit if you're not open.

I have spent so much of my life not being open as it pertains to my expectations. As I write this, I'm fully aware that it has cost me depth in my relationships. I've challenged myself to be open and available for people to deposit into my life even if that means being vulnerable. I challenge you to do the same. ***Vulnerability is the bridge that connects destiny and fulfillment.***

- **Be honest**! If you're going to successfully manage your expectations, one of the most important components is honesty. The truth is you have certain expectations for certain people and that's ok. You expect people close to you to be honest with you. You expect people to honor their commitments. You expect certain people to make you feel safe. The moment you begin pretending that you don't have certain expectations is the moment you begin building walls. Have you ever built walls around your feelings in effort to protect yourself from future hurt? If you're being *honest*, you'll likely admit the answer is a resounding, yes.

We've either done it or are currently doing it. ***You look at expectations as an opportunity for elevation, you'll stop running away from things that can emotionally lift you higher.***

- **Be Graceful**! It's going to happen - someone will let you down and/or hurt you emotionally. It may be intentional, which hurts even worse. I've come to realize first hand that the people who let you down do not do it intentionally. That's why it's important to practice being *graceful*. Recognize that no human being is perfect. People make mistakes and deserve forgiveness -- grace. I know I've made mistakes. I've dropped the ball in some friendships, in my parenting and even in my marriage at times. I've been the recipient of grace and it's encouraged me to show grace the same way it's been shown to me. In addition to that, it lightens the load that you

carry with you in your mind.

Chapter Four

Where Are You Headed?

"Hands out of the window and DO NOT make any sudden moves!"

I could barely make out what was said. I was trying to figure out exactly what was going on while trying not to make too many quick moves. About ten fully loaded semi-automatic pistols were pointing not just in my direction, but in the direction of every single person in the car. I placed my shaking hands out the window. I thought to myself, *How did I end up here? How did all of us end up here?*

Rewind back about two hours earlier. We were in my best friend Will's bedroom on an unusually warm

Can I Just Start Over?!

Saturday evening in the spring. In my city, there's never much to do, so we were trying to figure out what we could get into. That night, there were a few of us hanging. My self, Darian (aka DJ) and Will. The three of us could always be found together. Everyone called us, "The Three Amigos", we were inseparable. We did everything together, mostly causing mischief. We weren't just best friends, we were more like brothers.

DJ, who grew up in the same apartment complex with me, is literally one of the most lovable people I know. He's loved by just about everyone in our city, he's literally never met a stranger. For the record, I hate going out to eat with him. People of all ages and backgrounds end up coming to the table to talk while I'm trying to eat my chicken wings (if you see me at a wing spot, please say hi, just don't breathe on my wings).

Will is a super intelligent, down-to- earth, character whose loyalty and brotherhood is unmatched. You'll hear a little bit more about Will in a future chapter. However, for now, I'll say that he and his family have played such a vital role in my life. Oh yeah and he never leaves the house without being best dressed.

Also in the room was Brandon (aka Mumbles). Mumbles is a nickname he picked up from rec league basketball. Kyle, Will's step brother also made a rare appearance. Kyle was a different type of fellow. He was a combination of Christian Bale and Frank Sinatra, at least that's what he thought. He thought he was more mature and better than all of us. Weird fact, he wore dress slacks to school every day. Really though, who wears dress slacks to high school? Anyways that was Kyle.

Rounding out the crew that night was Mumble's girlfriend, who was on the way to pick us up in her two-door Honda Civic. Now, as I mentioned, we had nowhere to go. We sat in Will's bedroom playing Grand Theft Auto on Playstation 2, listening to Kanye West's debut album, College Dropout all while pointing a fully loaded BB gun at each other. We were ridiculous, but again, we had nothing going on. Nonetheless, she was on the way to pick us up and we were just going to go on a joy ride because that's what you do when you have nothing else to do. So, instead of riding around in a car that could potentially fit us all, we decided to ride around in a two-door Honda Civic. Yes, six people in a two-door car. But did it stop us? Of course not. We were all idiots.

We heard a car honking the horn, it was our ride. Something in the pit of my stomach that night said, *Why don't you just hang back? Why don't you just relax? Why don't you just do nothing?* I know I should've listened, but I proceeded to the door. We were all joking, pushing each other. DJ, being the bully of the group, says, "I got shotgun," which is code for "I'm sitting in the front," so that left Will, Mumbles, Kyle and myself in a back seat that was only really designed for two people. We were packed tight, like a can of sardines. "Where are we going?" someone asked. "I don't know. Just drive" said Mumbles.

We immediately put in a CD to provide a soundtrack for the night. I don't know about you, but my friends and I had a soundtrack for everything. We were riding around the city bumping music and heading to Wendy's (the OG dollar menu. It remains my favorite dollar menu). We ordered what seemed like $200 dollars of Wendy's dollar menu food and ate while we drove around the city. We made our way downtown where a car pulled up beside us at a red light. The car had four or five guys in it. Of course, we thought it would be fun to mess with them. I rolled down the backseat window where we proceeded to yell obscenities to them. This was a car full of what appeared to be some geeky kids who would be scared of us. Turns out it was the opposite. They were savages! I repeat, SAVAGES. These guys not only rolled down their window, they jumped out. This was a moment where we had to make a decision: Do we fight, which I was always down for, or do we drive away?

Before a decision could be made, Will turned his head in the opposite direction and rolled up the window. I happened to look down and recognized something was on the ground in the car. Something that I didn't even remember that we brought along. It was the BB gun. I grabbed it and pulled it out to show the guys in the other car and said something along the lines of "What y'all n****s want to do? Huh? Give me the money." One of the young men in particular went through an alley instead of hoping back in the vehicle. Another one of them attempted to jump a fence but instead flipped over it and fell on his face. It was one of the funniest scenes I had ever witnessed in my life. We were laughing hysterically. DJ laughed so hard until he was crying. It was hilarious. Kyle, as uptight as he was, was laughing too. It was ridiculous. We were having so much fun, we thought, *let's go do this some more*. So, we continued riding around the city flashing the gun, having a great time.

About twenty minutes later we came down one of the larger hills in the city. I happened to look in the rear view mirror and saw flashes of red and blue. At that moment, I didn't realize the gravity of the situation and the sheer stupidity of what we were doing or what was about to happen. I did however, take the BB gun, leaned over and threw it out of the window. Will screamed because that was his brand new gun. They hadn't yet recognized that the cops were on us. Around the very moment the gun hit the ground, cops pulled in front of us as well as behind us. So I asked the question in the beginning of this chapter, "How did we get here?" Well...that's how.

Several officers hoped out of their cars with guns drawn. One of the officers said, "Hands out of the window". The officers summoned us out of the car, one at a time. DJ opened the passenger side door for me with his right hand. As we got out of the car, the police ordered us to put our hands on our heads and take steps backwards. I saw a barrage of officers grab and throw my friends to the ground, one by one: DJ, Kyle, Mumbles, his girlfriend and Will. The bravado that I had earlier was now gone. In this moment, I was beyond nervous, I was flat out petrified. Time was happening in slow motion. That's what about a half dozen fully loaded guns drawn on you makes you feel like.

Each of us were handcuffed and led to sit on the curb. We were completely ignorant to the position we put ourselves and the officers in. Given the times we're living in today, we've seen videos of officers accidentally and sometimes intentionally shooting people. We could have ended up being victims that night and it would have been our fault.

We happened to be in one of the busiest areas of our city, so now we had dozens of onlookers watching us being taken out of the car, handcuffed and sitting on the side of the curb. It was the first time I was ever placed in handcuffs (and the last). I had no idea what I was going to do. What I did know was I was scared as hell to tell my mom. The officers were slowly but surely taking us by ourselves to ask us what was going on. Now at this point, I could only imagine or assume that each of us was being asked about the gun. Someone had told the police officers that a group of kids riding around in a white Civic were pointing a gun at people. It was a BB gun, but nonetheless, the officer grabbed me, looked me in my face and asked, **"where are you headed"**? I said, "Excuse me?" He repeated very long and drawn out, "Where are you all headed?"

That was a question that I couldn't answer, because I had no idea where I was headed that night. On a deeper level, it was a question about the direction I had been going my whole life. Just like I didn't realize where I was headed that night, I had no idea where I was headed in general. For me, that moment was life-altering. It was my wake-up call. I had just brandished what appeared to be a loaded firearm in the face of several people. *I realized that if you don't know where you're going any road can lead you there and you'll always end up at a place you don't want to be*.

As you skim the pages of this book, read the stories of my life and lessons I've learned, the question for you is *do you know where you're going? Do you know the direction that you're trying to take your life*? If you don't know, you're going the wrong way. There is nothing more powerful than knowing where you're going and being focused on the journey, knowing how to get to your destination and not wasting any energy while on your path. That night was all- encompassing of what my life was. I had the vehicle to take me wherever I wanted to go, but I didn't plug the destination into the GPS. Is that you? You're talented, you're gifted, you have tools, you have resources but you're still without a destination. So many of our lives are out of control. So many of us are spending time driving around in circles, getting lost, getting flat tires, figuratively, because we lack direction to take us to our desired destination.

Where do you want to go? Where are you going when you close the book? Where are you going when you wake up in the morning? Where are you leading yourself? Where are you leading your family? Where are you leading your life? A question I've started to ask myself on a very regular basis is *Rousawn, where are you going in your faith, family, finances and fitness?* It's important that you are successful in not just some, but all of these areas.

People put up their goals every year. They want to lose weight, but they neglect to take care of themselves in multiple ways . I'm an unapologetic Christian. Am I trying to convert you in this book? No. If this book inspires you to change your belief system, God bless. However, even if not, I still want to challenge you. What is your spiritual conditioning?

Have you found that thing inside of you that feels like there's something much bigger than you?

The officer picked us up. "We've heard you were pointing a gun at people. Where's the gun?" Have you ever heard the saying, "Snitches get stitches?" Well, there were no stitches given out that night because the entire crew stayed solid. We did stupid things together, so we'd go down together. I don't condone lying to cops, but I do condone being loyal to your friends and to those you love. Even more important is knowing where you're going in life.

Have you ever taken a look at the maps on the walls of rest stops? If you look closely enough, you'll likely find a star on the map with the words "you are here" written on it. When I know where I am, I can determine the roads I want to take to get to where I want to go. So, this is your rest stop moment. This is your moment to identify where you are and then find the roads and the vehicle to take you where you're going this time. That moment is now.

Oh, you're probably wondering what happened with the cops and gun situation that night. After searching the car inside and out, the cops found no evidence of a gun, thank God. Believe it or not, this is one of many crazy nights out that we had together. After the encounter, we were released and free to go. We knew we'd been extra lucky that night. We surely didn't tell our parents until many years later.

Chapter Five

1.9

"Come in and have a seat," said my high school principal. I was no stranger to being in the principal's office. It was a pretty usual occurrence between skipping school, not doing my homework, or just getting into mischief in general. I found myself there pretty often, but this day was different. It felt different. His tone was different. His face was different. Typically, he was pretty friendly with me. But this time I heard seriousness in his voice and not to mention, sadness in his eyes. It was almost as if he felt bad about what he was getting ready to say. At this point, I was a senior in high school. I had no idea where I was going in the next season of my life. I had managed to coast through and pretty much be the worst student possible, not because I was dumb, but because *I lacked direction, and when you lack direction, destruction always waits on the other side* (basically what we covered in the last chapter).

There I was, sitting across from my school's principal, a short guy with glasses who wasn't big into confrontation. He asked me a question: "Sean, what do you want?" Four words. One simple question for which I had no answer. I didn't even know what I wanted for lunch, let alone what I wanted in life. He asked, "Do you want to graduate?" I replied, "Do I want to graduate? Of course, I want to graduate", I replied. "I can't wait to get out of here". Once again, I still had absolutely no idea where I was headed. I was just ready to get out of high school, ready to live life, ready to see whatever life had in store for me. He pulled from his desk a piece of paper. All I could see was there was obviously something written on one side, the side he could see. He flipped it on its face and slowly slid it toward me. "What's that"? I asked.

He said, "Flip it over. You'll see." I flipped it over and tried to make out what it was. It looked like a report card, but it wasn't. It was my transcript. Immediately, my gut dropped. In the top right corner was my cumulative GPA or grade point average. My cumulative grade point average, also known as my overall grade point average, consisted of my average from my freshman year to halfway through my senior year. I glanced at it. I saw the number, and I was embarrassed. However, I can't say it surprised me. I simply said, "Okay."

"Do you want to graduate?" said my principal, again.

"Huh? Yes sir.? My voice took a humble tone.

"Well, look. You won't graduate with your peers." he said.

All of a sudden, all of the moisture left my mouth and went directly into my hands. As my heart started to pound, there was a trembling in my voice.

"What?" I said with confusion.

"What's your cumulative GPA, Sean?," he said rhetorically. To this day I still can't believe it. It took everything I had to utter it out of my mouth, "*1.9*."

Yeah, that's not a typo. You're reading it correctly. 1.9 cumulative overall GPA. That was the grade I had earned from my freshman year to my senior year. It wasn't even a C average in high school. Come on. Let's be honest. It's not that difficult to earn a 2.0 in high school. You practically have to try to do badly to get anything less, which is what I did. I just wasn't coming to school. I did just enough to be eligible for football and basketball. I did just enough to hang on by the skin of my teeth. Just enough not to get kicked out of school. *But just enough is never enough*. My eyes filled with tears. Understanding the gravity of what was happening for the first time ever, I sat in that seat, the seat I had become very familiar with, a seat that I had been in dozens of times, but this time I thought about my life twelve months from that moment and where I would actually be and I couldn't see anything. In fact, I couldn't even think about what I was going to do from that point on. I told the principal, "I want to graduate." He said, "I've tried to help you for the past two years. Unfortunately, you've been unwilling to help yourself, and *at some point, it doesn't matter how much someone else wants something, you have to be willing to help yourself.* Now we may be able to come up with some alternatives so that you can get your diploma this summer, but you will not graduate and receive your diploma the night of graduating with your peers."

He continued: "What makes me even more sad for you, Sean, is that you have to share this news with your mother." At that point, the tears that had been building up in my eyes began to stream down my cheeks. The rapid heartbeat turned to an immediate heartache. The hands that were sweating were now trembling, not from fear, but from an overwhelming sense of shame. I was ashamed not because I had let myself down, yet again. The woman who had sacrificed so much for me, who was willing to do whatever she had to do to see to it that I was succeeding. The woman who walked to work, the woman who would go without meals, the woman who ensured she'd do whatever she needed to give me whatever I needed.

The same strong-minded woman you learned about earlier in this book was no longer as strong in body. After months of thinking she was going to die, she had recently been diagnosed with terminal kidney failure. Her daily routine consisted of multiple dialysis treatments while still trying to work. I watched the weight fall from her body, like leaves fall from autumn trees. She was no longer the same outgoing person people had come to know and expect. She was sick and essentially dying. Now, I had to go home and give her news that would break any ounce of spirit she had left in her. I had no idea what to do next, but I had a decision to make. Whose fault was it that I had gotten to this point? It wasn't just my fault. Was this my father's fault? Was this my mother's fault? Was this the fault of unforeseen circumstances or the hand that I was dealt as a kid? It was so much easier for me to point the finger at others and at my life's circumstances rather than acknowledging the role I played in my failure. The truth is I wasn't being the best version of myself. I wasn't only failing in school, I was failing in life. It was just easier for me to point the finger of blame. That's what we do sometimes. *We blame people for our reality, thus relinquishing all power to make necessary changes.*

I got myself together, gathered my book bag, and walked out of the principal's office and instead of going to fourth period, I resorted back to my normal habits. I made my way out of the door, past the gymnasium to the student parking lot, got in my car, and I went home.

I didn't know what to do. I just knew that at that particular time, my mother was probably at work, and I'd have some time to relax at home before deciding what I was going to do next. It was unbearable. The feeling of shame set in. It was almost too much to bear. I brought all of this upon myself. Knowing that I skipped school, I didn't see a way to get myself out of the situation. I pulled into my driveway, parked the car into the garage, walked into the basement to my room. I took off my book bag and retrieved the transcript from my back pocket and looked at it, hoping for whatever reason that my GPA would have magically changed to a 2.9. Nope. Still a 1.9. Still a D average. Still going nowhere fast. I plopped down on the bed, closed my eyes and thought about what I was going to do. For the first time in my life, I felt completely hopeless. I didn't see a way to fix my situation, so I began to write down why I was mad and who I was mad at.

It was my mom's fault because when I was younger, she didn't make sure my dad was in my life everyday. I didn't know how to play sports when I was younger. I didn't know how to fix things (I still don't). I didn't know how to lead. I didn't know how to be a man and for those reasons, I was also mad at my dad. I didn't think he even cared. I didn't think he wanted anything to do with me on a personal and intimate level. It was my stepdad's fault too. It was my family's fault. It was everyone's fault, except mine.

I didn't take an ounce of ownership for my situation. That's right, *ownership*. I'm sure there are things you're walking through or wounds that haven't healed; if you have a heavy heart; if you're still dealing with something that happened twenty years ago or even twenty days ago, it's imperative that you take ownership. **Taking ownership is how you keep the power**. Casting blame and pointing the fingers causes you to relinquish power. I want you to know this, *taking ownership doesn't mean that what you've experienced or what you walked through is your fault. It just means that you're not going to allow it to control* *you.* Subconsciously, I allowed my experiences to control me and to have power over me as opposed to dealing with them. I ran from responsibility. *I ran from being my best self, and the further and faster I ran, the bigger the problems became.*

I was holding a 1.9 cumulative GPA. I became the person that I didn't want to be because I didn't take ownership of where I was or how I had gotten there. **What you refuse to own will soon own you,** and I was being owned. I remember at one time having aspirations of going to college, aspirations of being the first person in my family to graduate from a four-year university and maybe even going to get a master's degree. I wanted a job that would allow me to provide for my family and take care of people who needed help. But I was so far from that not because of my poor decision making but because I refused to take ownership. I laid there angry and upset.

Can I Just Start Over?!

For the first time ever in my life, the question of, *'would it be better for me not to live?'* crossed my mind. Would it be better if I were just gone? How could I possibly look my mother in the eyes and say that I didn't do my part? My mother was on some pretty strong pain medicine at the time. I thought, *Maybe I'll just take these pills, go to sleep, and never wake up.*

Rather than deal with how I was feeling, it would be easier to escape the reality that I'd created for myself. I walked up the stairs, back to the hallway and my parents' room. As I write this, I can still vividly see the light pink carpet and slanted ceiling in my parent's bedroom. The bed was made, as if my mother had just gotten up and left. I walked into the bathroom and opened the medicine cabinet. I took a bottle, placed it in my pocket, and walked downstairs to my room. I walked into my bathroom and flipped on the light. I looked myself directly in the eyes holding the prescription bottle in my hand. A feeling of relief crept up from my toes to the crown of my head and I began to weep uncontrollably. The tears felt liberating because I was looking at the person who caused the hurt. I was looking at the person who created his own reality. I was looking at the person who was responsible for where he was, but I felt liberated because I was also looking at the person who could make a decision to change the course of his life. I was looking at a person who had everything he needed to be successful. I was looking at the person that could turn things around.

What do you see when you look in the mirror? Do you see a victim? Are you looking at the person who was abused when they were younger? Are you looking at the person whose spouse walked out and now you have no control, or are you looking at the person who squandered the family's money and claimed bankruptcy? Or maybe you're looking at the person who refuses to be a prisoner of the past and wants to take the power back?! I can tell you -- you're looking at a victor when you see yourself in the mirror! When I looked at myself in the mirror that day, having my mother's pills in my pocket, I was at a fork in the road. Go left and end it all or take the road on the right, the longer more difficult path, however, it was the path of my destiny. Today, as you read this, I'm still on that path. Some days are better than others but I will forever be grateful for making the decision to press on.

They say hindsight is 20/20. I find it ironic that once we've walked through something, we can clearly see solutions and things we could have done differently. That's definitely the case for my cumulative GPA in highschool. So much so that I've created a cool little acronym that if applied can help you take action and design the future you desire. It's called **GPA**. Let's walk through it.

'G' stands for **goals.** What goals do you have for your life? Really take a moment to evaluate your goals and dreams. At the time I was failing high school, I had no big tangible goals. The problem with that is, *when you're aiming at nothing, you'll hit the mark every single time.* Giving yourself clear goals, enables you to measure the effectiveness of your actions.

The **'P'** stands for **positioning.** The *verb* definition for position means *to put or arrange (someone or something) in a particular place or way.* Once you've established clear goals it's important to position yourself in the right places and with the right people. I often found myself out of position which is why I was often out of balance. Where do you need to be positioning yourself right now? Are the rooms in which you're in preparing you for where you want to go? Also, are the people you're spending time with propelling you forward or are they pressing pause on your progress?

The **'A'** in our acronym stands for **accelerate**. I'm still amazed by how an object the size of a Boeing 747 can take off and fly through the air for hours. The funny thing is that my favorite part about flying isn't the flight itself, it's the takeoff. In order for the plane to successfully take flight, it must *accelerate* to high speeds on the runway. The same is true for your life. In order to fly and reach the level of your potential, you must gain some momentum aka *acceleration*. You can gain massive acceleration by consistently staying on track with your *goals* and *positioning*. When this acronym is used successfully, you'll 'takeoff' towards your dreams!

You are the person who can make a difference, beginning today. That's the power of pure, unadulterated ownership. It says, "this may not totally be on me but, I'll own it. I take responsibility because as long as I have responsibility for it, I have a hand in altering the direction in which I'm going".

*If you or someone you know is batteling thoughts of suicide, please contact the **National Suicide Prevention Lifeline** 1-800-273-8255.*

You are not alone. People love you and will fight with you.

Can I Just Start Over?!

Chapter Six

I Am Not Your Booty Call

There were hundreds of people around me screaming, yelling, laughing, focusing on a basketball game, yet I sat in a daze, just a couple of days removed from my principal telling me I was not graduating. On the outside, I pretended that everything was great. I was still the jokester. The entertainer in me still wanted to make people laugh, but on the inside, I was completely devastated. Suddenly, the sound of the buzzer snapped me back into reality. The first half of the basketball game was over, and I had seventy-two dollars in profit in my pocket. Since I stopped playing basketball, I didn't go to the basketball games to watch. I couldn't see why

112

people would do that. Being a natural born hustler and entrepreneur, I went to make money. How? Well, gambling, of course.

I would bet people about random things like which player would come off the bench first; who would make the first basket; which team would make the next basket. I would go up and down the student section collecting bets, taking money, cashing in or paying out. It became something people looked forward to. They would bring mountains of cash to the game just to gamble. It was incredible. I probably made a couple of grand that season. This was my first game back after having been kicked out three games prior for gambling. Anyway, as the second quarter was getting ready to start, I had $172 in my pocket. That was enough money for me to have a good time immediately following the game. That is, if I didn't lose it while gambling in the second half.

At the time, $172 was a lot of money to spend with my partner in crime, my best friend, DJ. Not only were we out for the night, but we had DJ's mom's Chevy Malibu. What? We felt unstoppable. With money and a car, the possibilities were limitless. At the end of the game (all of my money still intact), we walked down out of the gymnasium towards the parking lot. However, I've since retired from gambling because I'm not very good...at all. We were hanging out trying to figure out what we were going to get into that night. We talked to a couple of people. There was a party going on across town. There were people going out to eat. So many things to do, so many possibilities, so much money, at least we thought.

There was a young lady I was talking to at the time, well a couple of young ladies. One of them in particular wanted me to go out to eat with her and her friends. I didn't necessarily want to go, but I figured I owed her that much at least. I had stood her up a couple of weeks prior. Just as we got into the Malibu, I got a phone call from my mom. She said she needed me to come home to help her out with something. We only lived a couple of miles away from the gym, so DJ and I drove to my house blasting one of my favorite artists, Rick Ross, singing his latest hit, "Where My Money".

That night we thought we were balling. Between the two of us, we had about $200. We pulled up to my house. I went inside. My mother warned me with a sense of humor to stay out of trouble, suggesting that we were used to getting in trouble. Okay. She was right. We did get into things that we shouldn't have. A couple of minutes later, I went back down to my room, and DJ was on the phone. He seemed to be upset and emotional. "Hey, what's going on?" I asked.

"We need to go find my brother". He told me his
brother was about to get into a fight. We needed to
leave. I'll be honest. Fighting was something we liked
to do, not like fighting in the gym or boxing, but street
fighting.

I knew what time it was. I changed my shoes. We
hopped in the Chevy Malibu and off we went. We
went to the location where the fight was supposed to
be, but nobody was there. We spent the next fifteen to
twenty minutes trying to contact everybody who would
be around them, and we got nothing. So now, instead
of going out to eat and meeting the young lady I said I
would meet, we rode around town for fifteen minutes,
then thirty minutes, then forty-five. Soon, an hour
passed, Finally, we pulled over. It was time to switch
plans. I asked, "Yo, what are we going to do tonight"?
I was starving. I said, "Look, just take me by
Applebee's." I would at least go in to see the young

lady, say hi. I asked DJ to take me back to the house to get my good shoes back on. So, we went back to my house. My mom was in the living room. She asked if we were staying out of trouble. We told her we were. Of course, it was a lie. We were looking to get into trouble, but still we hadn't gotten into trouble yet. I grabbed my shoes and got back in the car. About fifteen minutes later, we pulled into Applebee's parking lot.

DJ asked if I wanted him to come in with me. I told him he might as well. We could go inside and eat at the bar. Keep in mind we weren't even eighteen yet, talking about sitting at the bar. We got out of the car and as our feet hit the pavement to go into Applebee's, I heard a familiar voice. A voice that in the past would annoy the crap out of me.

Out of the door walked two young ladies that both DJ and I knew, one of whom DJ and I grew up with in the apartment complex, her name was Nikki. She was with one of her best friends, Michelle - a young lady I met in sixth grade when we began going to the same middle school. In fact, Michelle actually dated me for a day and then broke up with me, but that's not important (another eye roll right here...nope actually a stank face). The first words out of Michelle's mouth was NOT, "Hey Sean, nice to see you. Hope all is well." No. Instead, she blurted out, "What girl are you here to see tonight?". How could she assume that I was coming to talk to a girl? She was exactly right. There are two things that I cared about in high school: ball—that would be a football—and booty. Now, I'm not talking about the booty that pirates steal. Nope, I'm embarrassed about it, but that's who I was. I cared about ball and booty and towards the end of my high school career, I cared about booty more than ball. So, I answered Michelle's question. I told her the name of the young lady I was there to see, and she rolled her eyes. She proceeded to leave. She said it was too crowded at Applebee's, so she and Nikki were going across the street to eat. I thought she was going to ask us if we wanted to join them. When she didn't, I asked if we could tag along. When she said she didn't mind, I went inside Applebee's to speak to the young lady I was supposed to have dinner with. She had saved me a seat and seemed quite excited. I stayed long enough to say hello and then told her I had to go home because I wasn't feeling well. That was one of the last times we'd talk. Yes, I lied. It wasn't good. But I had to get to the Outback that just so happens to be out front of Applebee's.

Hanging out with Michelle and Nikki that night was so refreshing. I had known these girls just about my entire life, so I didn't have to play "Mr. Smooth" or "Mr. Cool Guy." I could just be myself. Everyone could be themselves, so we had one of the most incredible evenings. It was cool. It was a different type of vibe. Most young ladies don't like to eat all the food in front of guys. They try to be cute. They will say something like, "Oh no, I'm not that hungry." But Michelle ate more than DJ and I and that says a lot.

As we got ready to leave, I asked Michelle and Nikki where they were headed. There was a brief moment of silence, and then Michelle said she was going back to her mom's house. Her folks were out of town. I asked, "Can we come over?"...... silence. They looked at each other and said, "Okay, for a little bit." They hopped in their car and DJ and I hopped in the Malibu and were on our way to Michelle's house. Now, I can't remember much about the conversation that DJ and I had, but what I do know is that we thought it was going to be a good night. This was 2006, so there was no such thing as Netflix, but we did watch a movie, which is always cool. Michelle got up from the couch and went into the kitchen. Three minutes later she came back and sat down with a plate of cheese fries. She asked DJ and I if we wanted some, and of course, we said "Yes." Little did I know, we were indulging on my leftover cheese fries. I mean, the audacity of this girl to heat up my food (insert angry face emoji lol). As the movie was about to end, I figured I'd go in for the kill. I'd take a shot. It was do or die, now or never. So being the lady's man that I was, I slid over, placed my hand on her shoulders in a smooth way, and I went in for the kiss on her neck, a classic move in which I had always been successful. As soon as my lips got about a half inch from her neck, she abruptly moved away, looked at me dead in the eye, and asked, "What are you doing?" "Nothing," I said, "I was just trying to smell what type of perfume you had on". "It's called soap and water", she replied. Wow, deined.

Having been denied, my ego was damaged, but I was actually up for the challenge. Two minutes later, I slid in a little bit closer, put my hand on her leg, about an inch above the knee cap. Then I slowly began to move my hand a little higher and a little higher. Just as I thought I was going to hit the jackpot, she grabbed my hand, but not in an intimate way. I'd describe it as an arm-wrestling squeeze. She looked me in the eyes and said these words, "*I am not your booty call*". Six words; six simple words. It was the way she said them and how she said them that changed my life. "*I am not your booty call*". I was aware in that moment of all the emotion I had from not graduating high school on time, all of the shame I felt, all of the hurt I was carrying, all of the frustration with being denied and put in my place - what it was like to *have a standard of excellence for yourself.* Up until that point, I had struggled to have a standard of excellence for myself that required me to be greater.

When you have a standard of excellence for yourself, it doesn't matter what other people are doing. It doesn't matter what they expect of you because your expectation for yourself trumps theirs. I remember her letting my hand go. I took my hand and put it in my pocket. I wasn't embarrassed. I was encouraged, inspired even. No other girl had ever said that to me. She was different. She cared about herself. She had values. She had morals, and when a person has values, morals, and a standard for themselves, they don't let anything less than that around them. That's why I was in the situation I was in: I didn't truly value myself - I walked around with a false sense of confidence and an inflated ego.

The truth is that booty call denial saved my life. It forced me to reconsider my standards. Never before did I have a standard for myself, intellectually or emotionally. My character was highly flawed. I didn't respect my body. I had not respected other young women, but now, unbeknownst to her, Michelle helped me realize something. I believe God sent her into my life at that very moment, to change my perspective and outlook on everything. I believe had it not been for Michelle, God's unique and divine intervention in my life through her memorable "I am not your booty call" statement, I'd be in a completely different place.

Fast-forward fourteen years. I'm writing this book, and I just had a play session with my two daughters, Alayah and Abrie. They couldn't be more adorable. Alayah's heart is so pure, so open, so emotional. She wears it on her sleeve. She's also inquisitive and intellectually curious. Abrie is so emotionally tough and strong. Yet, she's extremely loving and affectionate. I have so much love for my girls. I think about what I want for them, what I want for their future. I don't want them to have a man in their life like I was in high school. I want them to have a man that cares about them and respects them and loves them and values them.

Just being real, having my own two daughters now makes me feel repentant for how I treated young ladies back in high school. So because it's my book, and I can say what I want: if you and I had a relationship in the past and you're reading this book (which is a longshot), you probably don't like me much. But if you're reading any of this, *I sincerely apologize for not treating you like the woman of God that you are. I'm sorry for not valuing you, for not respecting you, for not speaking life over you and encouraging you. I am truly sorry and I hope that you'll forgive me.* Now, back to the book.

Michelle changed my life. She became my wife. I knew from the moment she said those words to me that I wanted her in my life. So there was only one thing to do. I had to invite her to Shoney's the very next day after we hung out that night. My mom and I were going to Shoney's (the best breakfast spot of all time). That next morning, she stepped out of her white Pontiac Sunfire wearing a miniskirt and white Reebok classics. Oh my goodness. I didn't deserve it. But God had sent me a gift and from that day, we'd become best friends. She's been with me through the best of times, and the worst of times. And though she won't admit it, without her, you wouldn't be reading this book.

It all came down to the standards of excellence she had for herself. She knew where she was going, and not only did she know where she was going, she knew the quality of people who were going there with her. That day at Shoney's she talked about going to college. She asked me, "Where are you going to college?" As much as I wanted to be honest with her, I couldn't tell her that I wasn't going to be graduating with my peers and that our principal had worked out a way for me to go to summer school every single day in order for me to get my diploma. When I finally did share that with her, not only did she not leave, she was supportive. She helped me to raise my standards. She woke up every single day and drove me to summer school, dropped me off and picked me up. Not to mention, she stood in line several times to buy me Jordan's (God, would you mind nudging her spirit to buy me J's again?). She didn't just tell me she wanted me to succeed. She put skin in the game. She invested in me. She helped me get my finances together. I had a negative balance in my bank account. She sold her prom dress to help me cover that. Again, she had standards. She knew where she was going. She wanted me to go, but she refused to allow the existing version of me to tag along.

Let me ask you, *what are your standards*? What standards and expectations do you have for yourself--not the standards that people have for you, but what standards do you have for yourself? Because surely, and surely I tell you that there will be times when people don't think you can make it, but it's not about what they think. It's about the standards and expectations you have for yourself.

Your standards for yourself have to be higher than the ones others have for you. I found that out through *Michelle*. When you understand your own standards, you understand the standards and the quality of people you want in your life. That's not to say that you don't converse or associate with people who don't value things that you value or have the same standards that you have, but you cannot continue to give people energy that don't have a high standard for themselves because they will eventually take what energy you have. *People emulate the energy you radiate*.

And then what do you expect out of life? At a young age, Michelle valued herself enough to say, "I'm not your booty call." That translates to "I'm not coming down to your level now. You can come up to mine". Whatever it is you've been going through, you are going to become the master of your mindset beginning right now. Say to yourself, "hey, I know what I'm capable of. I know where I'm going and I'm not going to allow anyone or anything to knock me off of the standard I have for myself".

Michelle - thank you for taking a shot on me over 14 years ago. Just being honest with you, I don't know that I'd allow Alayah or Abrie to risk their future on a young man that was in my position. You didn't listen to the naysayers nor did you ever do anything but encourage me to get better on a daily basis. You're more than my wife, you're my best friend and life partner. Hundreds of thousands of people will read this book not because I'm special but because of your investment in me. To say I'm grateful would be grossly understated. I love you and guess what....we're just getting started.

Chapter Seven

Keep Pedaling

I felt the wind in my face. I was riding faster than I ever had. I remember my mother saying to me, "Son, keep pedaling". At that moment, I realized she had taken her hand off of the seat and that the reason I was riding faster than I ever had was because she pushed me. In a matter of seconds, I was on the ground. I crashed hard, and I'm not just talking about a little bit. I mean, I hit the ground so hard, I bounced up and landed again. Well, I know falling down is part of learning how to walk, or ride, in this case.

Pain is a part of life, but it sucks. It sucks when you just want to ride and feel the wind in your face or in the case of everyday life, you just want to live life to the fullest and have experiences that are awesome and memories you can share, but you end up on the ground bleeding. My mother rushed over to my eight-year-old body. I had a bloody knee and elbow. She helped me up and told me, *"If you're going to learn how to ride, you need to get back on the bike and keep pedaling."* That is how you learn how to ride. She said, "Gather yourself, brush yourself off, look in the direction that you want to go and pedal!"

Keep your eyes on where you want to go and you peddle in that direction. Three simple steps:

- *Gather yourself*
- *Look in the direction you want to go*
- *Pedal in that direction*

No one believed that I could ride more than my mother, not just in the case of the eight-year-old

Rousawn on a bike, but my entire life. She was my number one cheerleader of course until Michelle came along. No matter what I was doing, whether it was baseball, which I was terrible at; basketball, which I was pretty good at, or football, she believed that if I could keep my composure, see where I wanted to go, and pedal in that direction, then I could get there.

What's crazy is that she believed in me athletically, but she also believed in me emotionally and intellectually. You've read the book. You've gotten to this chapter. There was no way that anyone should have had faith that a young man with a 1.9 cumulative GPA in high school. Let alone could he ever have college-level dreams. My mother believed that I could do whatever I put my mind to, and that delirious optimism is what allows me to live and dream big. Who would ever have thought that I would be an author? What I came to know at a young age is that if I could just believe in myself, I could become anything that I wanted, but I didn't believe in myself. All the things that I'd done up until that point almost convinced me that I wasn't meant to go any further. After Michelle spent months personally driving me to summer school, I finally received the diploma that my classmates got on graduation night. I had to take an Algebra I class the summer following my senior year. As I mentioned, Michelle made sure I got there every single day.

My sister Kayla, Michelle, and I went to Marshall University, five hours away from home. Well, Kayla and Michelle went to Marshall University. It was by the grace of God, I was able to get into Marshall University Community College, which happened to be on the same campus as Marshall University.

I believed that in less than a few weeks I would

probably be back home. I had very little faith that I

could complete college, but guess who believed? Yes,

my mother did. I would spend the mornings before my

first class having breakfast with Michelle. I would see

her off to class and would walk through the middle of

the Marshall University campus talking to my mother

on the phone, describing to her how college was

going. I would highlight features of the campus: the

fountain that commemorates and honors all the

victims of a 1970 plane crash. I talked to her about

what was going on in the cafeteria, etc. She said

speaking with me in the mornings encouraged her

spirit. Truth is, I was talking to her for encouragement.

It really was important for me to be affirmed by her

and receive emotional support.

Yet, at the same time, I was paralyzed by my past

decisions and I needed to be pushed into my

potential. Just as she had pushed me on a bike toward where I was going. I almost needed that same push to go in a direction of where God was calling me, and it was her encouragement that did that. There's nothing wrong with receiving support from others. It's important. Some of us didn't receive the encouragement we needed as kids. Some of us as young people didn't get words of affirmation spoken over us. Sometimes, you're just going through a mess, and you need someone to remind you of what you're capable of. *Don't downplay encouragement.* Don't act as if you're too tough or too strong-minded to get encouragement because no matter how tough you are, ***the right words from the right person can help you move in the right direction***.

It is through encouragement that I would receive the right words from the right person. There were times where I felt so stupid because I attended community college rather than the university, but my mom and Michelle both would encourage my spirit. They would remind me of how far I'd come to get to where I was. They would tell me if I just did my work at the community college level, the following year I would get accepted into the main university. Not only were they right, they were so right they were wrong. It didn't take the entire year to get into the university. After the first semester at Marshall Community College, I was accepted into the university. My grade point average was so strong that they allowed me to transfer on to the university after just one semester, and that's because I had someone speaking to my potential instead of reminding me of my past. I hope that as you read this book, you discern the type of people you have in your life.

Are the people you're surrounding yourself with speaking to your potential and what you're capable of, or are they reminding you of your past and what you've been through?

For my Bible lovers who are reading this, we know in scripture it says that *it is better to give than to receive.* My mother was a giver (not in the Biblical since per say. I don't think she ever tithed, traditionally). She felt better when she gave energy away. She felt better when she was giving compliments or encouragement. She wasn't one to want to receive a lot. In fact, the time that she was giving me encouragement and hope was the time that she needed them most herself. As I mentioned in earlier, she had been diagnosed with kidney failure. She was hooked up to a dialysis machine. She had lost between fifty and sixty pounds. Her skin had darkened; her hair had fallen out. Essentially, she was in need of a kidney.

I had volunteered to give her a kidney. I mean, it was the least I could do. She had made so many sacrifices for me as a boy. She never would have taken it. She never did take it. She'd continue to be my support system, my biggest fan. She would tell everybody how proud she was of the fact that her son, the son that she had when she was young, the son she raised in section 8 housing, the son that people had given up on and didn't believe that he was going to make something of himself, was in college. She'd say things like, "he's going to provide for his family and be a blessing to others". She saw those things when I didn't see them. I can remember how much I wanted to make her proud. Not only did I want to get a 3.0, which was my goal for the longest time and achieved, but I wanted to achieve even more. I wanted to be on the Dean's list, and I wanted to bring her the certificate and say, "Mom, we did it. Look what we achieved!"

Can I Just Start Over?!

In our junior year, Michelle and I got our first college apartment. It was the coolest thing. We had our own space. We had our own stuff. We even got a dog, Max (what's up my first born son...wait you can't read). I remember inviting my mom down. She was so excited to come. We were concerned about whether or not she would be able to make the five hour trip. She was going to bring all of her dialysis supplies with her and spend the weekend with us. She called me the night before she was supposed to come. She had been diagnosed with shingles, and it would keep her from coming. But only fifteen or twenty seconds of that call was devoted to her disappointment. She spent the rest of the call encouraging me and reminding me that although the rest of my college career was going to be hard, I needed to stay focused on where I was going and to move in that direction.

It was just like my mom to be constantly giving, but what she didn't know is that I was working to give her something: that Dean's list certificate, and I was going to make it happen. I wasn't going to be distracted because I had bills to take care of now. I was going to make the Dean's list in spite of those responsibilities. So right before Christmas break, I'd refreshed my computer to find that I made the Dean's list with a 3.8 GPA. I shared the news with Michelle. We were excited. We made the drive home for Christmas break. The next morning, I was setting the table as my mom was preparing breakfast, and I shared the news with her. I saw the tears in her eyes. I'd seen tears running down her cheek before, but it was always because of her being disappointed with decisions I had made. These were tears of joy, tears of her being proud of her son. I couldn't wait to present my mom with the certificate. I didn't even want it. She cleared a space on her wall where she would put it. It would be symbolic of how far we'd come and a cornerstone for how high we were going to build the success we were going to have.

We enjoyed the rest of the Christmas break. On our last day in town, I sat down with mom and talked at length. We talked about life, talked about things that were stressing me, talked about things she was dealing with. We were getting ready to go into the year 2009. I remember how vivid the conversation was, how she was so optimistic and encouraged. She said 2008 had been such a hard year. She found herself in and out of the hospital with extended stays. Month after month she'd be doing well one day, and the next day she would have taken three steps back. She said, "son, I believe that 2009 is going to be the best year I've ever had." I said, "You know, mom? I'm with you". I needed it to be. I needed her to get healthy, get strong so together we could start living

the life that was destined for us. As I was leaving, I

hugged her and told her that I would give her a call.

When I prepared to leave, she stood on the porch. We

said, "I love you" to each other. As I drove up the

street a little bit, I stopped and took a glance in the

rearview mirror. I don't know why, but something told

me to position the mirror so that I could see her smile.

I was going back to school to continue to work toward

the goal we set to be the first person in my family to

graduate college. I saw that smile, how proud she

was, how optimistic she was. It was an incredible

feeling.

That night, I gave her a call once Michelle and I made

the five hour trip back to Huntington, WV. We talked

for a while before she started sharing with me some

things she was worried about for the future, not for

herself, but for certain people, certain decisions they

were making, certain things she wished for them and wanted for them and hoped for them. As we hung up, I felt something shift. I can't explain it, but the next day I got a call that through the night my mother had gotten sick. She started to throw up blood and was rushed to the hospital where the doctors tried to figure out what was going on. They looked to see if an infection had occurred in her kidneys, which was oftentimes the case. They couldn't find anything. The next day the doctors determined that the infection was septic and that they would have to do immediate surgery to try to fix it, but at that point her body was so weak. The surgeon called me. I was given a power of attorney over her in the event any decisions had to be made.

The surgeon said, "This is what's going on with your mother. She's septic. There's a procedure I would like to do, but there's only a three percent chance that her body can make it through this operation because of the status". "But if she doesn't get it," I said, "there's a hundred percent chance that she'll perish." I'll never forget the strength of Michelle who was holding my hand and physically supporting me to stand up as I made the decision to go through with the surgery. Thirty minutes later, I got a phone call from the same surgeon that my mother had passed away. Tears ran down my cheeks. Tears of pain, tears of agony. My mother, my best friend, was gone. How did we get here? What was I going to do? Do I even know how to ride this bike? Do I even know how to pedal if she's not behind me?

I came home to make funeral arrangements. It was just a few days away from the start of the spring semester. I can recall not wanting to go back to college. I wanted to take some time off to get my head right, and then I remembered what my mother would have wanted me to do. What was the goal? The goal was to be the first person in my family to graduate college. So, how I felt was no longer important. My perspective changed at that moment. *Perspective drives performance. When your perspective changes, you realize that it's not about how you feel, but it's more about what you are committed to.* That feeling I had when I said I was going to be the first person to graduate college was a great one. I was excited when I made that declaration to my mother, but now I was brokenhearted. I was hurt, angry, and sad. It was at that point I had to ask myself a critical question: *Are you going to be committed?, or are you going to allow the way you feel determine how you operate?* I said to myself, *You will be the first person in your family to graduate college.* That day I began to be driven by my performance. That mindset continues to this day. The loss I felt did not break me. It helped to mold me as a person as well as my passion for mindset development.

After my mom's funeral, Michelle and I got back in the car and we headed toward Huntington, WV. I was laser focused on the goal. When we arrived back home, I checked the mailbox. The Dean's List certificate had arrived. I couldn't give it to my mother. It had lost its original significance. It was supposed to have been our moment of celebration, a reminder of how far we had come, but the certificate had a slightly different meaning now. In my spirit that day it was a reminder of what I committed to doing and all those things my mom said I could achieve. It was a reminder that I wasn't just a little boy in section eight housing. It was a reminder that I wasn't just a young man with a 1.9 cumulative GPA. It was a reminder that if I believed in myself I could achieve anything I put my mind to. That piece of paper reminded me that my mother was right about me when she said I could accomplish anything.

My perspective drives my performance; I want you to know that you can accomplish anything. I want you to know that you have the capacity to accomplish great things; you are just a decision away from having everything you want. I say this not theoretically, but because I've lived it. I've been low, I've been high, and I've been low again, but what I know is just like that piece of paper reminded me that I'm capable of greatness, I'm here to remind you that you are capable of great things as well.

You may have had challenges, but no matter what you've been through, gather yourself. Take some time, be sad, shake it off. **Get your composure**. Get on your bike. **Look in the direction that you want to go** in, not the direction that people tell you that you should go, or the direction or the levels that they say you can get to, but the direction that you want to go, and I want you to **begin pedaling in that direction**. I'm not saying that you'll never fall again, but if you do fall, be sure to get back on your bike.

In memory of my mother, Laura Darlene Dozier. Your confidence and support of me is unmatched. I love you. PS...still very much a 'momma's boy'.

Chapter Eight

Hi, My Name Is Will

It was roughly 11:30 p.m. at night. My wife Michelle and I had to drop off a couple of things at my dad's house. Rather than staying there, we decided to go back over to her mom's house, get a good night's sleep before we packed up to head back to Huntington, WV the following morning. On the car ride, we were talking about how amazing our honeymoon to Jamaica was. The food was incredible, and we were so carefree. Everything about the honeymoon was beautiful. We came to a stop sign. My wife had a puzzled look on her face. I looked at her. She squinted more intently and focused on whatever had her attention. I asked, "What's going on?" She said, "Sean, is that Will?" I looked and said "Nah, can't be. It's too far out of the way. Pull up there and let me find out."

We don't recognize the magnitude of moments because sometimes they seem rather mundane. Let me tell you about when I first met Will in fourth grade. It was the first day of school and I walked into Ms. Chase's fourth grade classroom looking "so fresh." I had on my Jordan's, a fresh haircut with a part on the side. I was just trying to look nice, but as usual the teachers already knew what kind of student I was. I wasn't known for being the most well-behaved kid at school, so I walked in class and sat at the last desk in the last row.

Ms. Chase looked up and said, "Sean, why don't you come sit up here next to me?" signaling towards the desk directly in front of her. I said, "really?" I grabbed my book bag, and I marched toward the seat directly in front of her desk. You could hear the snickers and the giggles from the students. When I pulled back my seat and plopped down. The young man sitting next to me gave me the most welcoming and genuine smile I'd ever seen. He extended his hand toward me and said, *"Hi, my name is Will"*.

What appeared to be an insignificant, mundane moment was actually monumental. Not only did Will become my friend; he became one of my best friends. Scratch that. He became my brother. As I mentioned, God has sent people into my life strategically for reasons I didn't even realize. Will and his family are some of those people.

Will and I lived two completely different lifestyles. I lived in section 8 housing, didn't have a vehicle or much at all as it pertains to financial resources. Will grew up in a completely different world financially. But the one thing I can remember and appreciate so much is that Will and his mom, Julie, didn't care about that. I remember vividly Julie driving her brand new Mercedes into my apartment complex to pick me up. People would look at her car trying to make out who this crazy white woman was driving through our neighborhood. She drove through numerous times and had no fear of being robbed. That's the type of person she is. As I mentioned earlier, there are times you don't recognize the magnitude of moments because sometimes they seem rather mundane. Julie and Will may have believed that coming into the projects to pick me up was mundane, their actions were far from that...they were monumental. I was exposed to so much in those projects. I literally grew up twice as fast as the kids my age. Julie and Will allowed me to see parts of the world that I didn't know existed. In fact, Will's house was the first actual house I ever visited. I'm confident that my exposure to them helped me see things that I wanted for myself and family as I got older...*monumental moments.*

Will and I got into so much craziness it's probably best that I leave the details out of the book. We went through good times and bad times together, but one thing that remained the same was our bond and loyalty to each other. I was charismatic, outgoing, a little crazy at times. Will was the opposite: considerate, thoughtful and mature.

Will was probably the most selfless person I'd ever met. He would give you the shirt off his back, the food off his plate. I'm confident that through high school I spent more time at Will's house than my own. As I mentioned in previous chapters, DJ, Will and I were inseparable. However, by the middle of our senior year, we naturally started to go our separate ways for the first time. I started dating Michelle, who eventually became my wife. But as close as Will and I were, everything came to a head right around the time of our wedding.

My wife pulled into the convenience store to investigate whether or not the person that looked like Will was actually him. The closer we got, the harder it was to admit to ourselves that it was him. I did not want the person who I was looking at to be my best friend. The person that I was looking at was standing on the side of the entrance to a gas station. He was wearing a wifebeater, and he looked to be twenty-five pounds lighter than my friend was. His eyes were sunken and his skin looked bad. His teeth didn't look the best. His clothes looked like they hadn't been washed in weeks. He looked like *he* hadn't washed in weeks. That was not my friend Will who was always fresh, always clean, always wearing the best outfit, the best sneakers. This couldn't be my friend, but as much as I didn't want it to be, it was very much him.

Can I Just Start Over?!

Michelle pulled over and I got out of the car. Will and I locked eyes. He took a deep breath and just like that, Will proceeded to hug me like everything was all right.

I'm not going to hold any punches. I'm going to be real. People in my life that I've loved have struggled with substance abuse and alcoholism, but this was personal. Will had been struggling with drugs for years. His struggle with drugs kept him from being in my wedding. I remember the disagreement like it was yesterday. Something as simple as getting fitted for a tuxedo was almost impossible to mess up. However, when it was time to go get fitted, I could never track him down. Michelle was so nervous. It wasn't that she didn't want him in the wedding. She loved Will, but she didn't think we could rely on him. I didn't want that to be true. However, a couple of days before my wedding , I didn't hear from him and couldn't find him.

He couldn't even make it to the rehearsal, so at the last minute I had to replace him with somebody else.

I'm not blaming his addiction, but what I'm saying is addiction is real. Addiction will turn a person from who they used to be into a shell of themselves and into a person you can't recognize physically, emotionally, or mentally. Will, one of the most trustworthy people I'd ever known began stealing his mother's jewelry just to be able to get a fix.

Now, in front of the gas station, looking at him, he tried to put on a facade like everything was cool. I didn't recognize the person I was seeing. I heard a voice that sounded familiar, but I didn't feel the same spirit.

I asked him, "Are you good?" He said, "Yeah, I'm fine, man. I'm like... I'm doing good." Now, I was listening to him talking, but I couldn't receive it. I looked over my right shoulder. I looked at my wife's face and she looked lost, like she didn't know whether she wanted to save me or throw Will in the car and take him to get help. But just as I was looking at my wife, I saw a black car with tinted windows. The window was down, and there was a gentleman who was looking in Will's direction.

I looked at the guy. He said, "Can I help you?" I replied, "I don't know. Can you?" Will grabbed my arm, looked at me and said, "Sean, he's my ride." But because I know where I come from, I knew that wasn't his ride. That was a dope boy. He was there to sell to one of his customers. Understanding that something could have escalated outside of the car, Michelle asked me to please go into the store and get her something. I turned to Will to ask if he needed anything. He said he didn't and told me to call him the next day.

The next day, Michelle and I left to head back to Huntington. I was working now. We didn't really speak much of the interaction with Will. My heart hurt. That night, outside of the store, I wanted to talk to Will. I wanted to tell him I loved him, that I appreciated him. I wanted to tell him that I was proud of him and wanted better for him, but I didn't.

We would go months without talking on the phone. In fact, I still remember calling him a few months later and telling him that Michelle and I were pregnant. I remember him saying, "I'm going to be the coolest uncle". I assured him that he would be. He was so excited. He couldn't wait to meet my daughter. Michelle and I ended up moving back to Martinsburg. We wanted to be closer to family and friends so that we could spend more time with them. However, days turned to weeks, weeks turned into months and as much as I thought I'd be able to hang out with the people I loved, between being a full-time husband, father and employee, I never could find the time to spend as much time with my friends as I had before. Will had been reaching out a lot at that time.

Will and I had been connecting a lot. It was almost reminiscent of our high school days. He was sharing some future goals he had, I was doing the same. He had gone through rehab and had been doing well personally. The future seemed bright. He talked of wanting to go to school. It would have been easy for him. He remains one of the most naturally intelligent people I've ever met. Then sadly, a few weeks later, I heard of his relapse.

I worked about ten minutes from his house, and I still remember him telling me to stop by on this particular Saturday when I got off of work. I was tired and didn't really feel like it. I asked him if I could stop by the following week. He told me that was fine. He just wanted to tell me about his promotion at his job, Long John Silver's. I told him that was awesome. I have nothing against Long John Silver's, but I just knew I was talking to the smartest person I had ever known. He wanted to be a lawyer and a sports agent. A promotion at Long John Silver's didn't even come close.

Will wanted to meet our daughter, Alayah, but I couldn't bring myself to allow her to be around him because I didn't know what he was going through at the time. Not long after that my wife wanted to eat at Long John Silver's (how ironic). It didn't ever occur to me that Will might be there. When we went through the drive-through and put in our order. As we pulled up to the window, we saw Will's mom Julie's vehicle.

Michelle said, "Why don't you take Alayah inside to meet Will?" There's been a couple of times in my life when my wife has said something and everything on the inside of me said, "Listen" but for whatever reason I fought it. I said, "No, she's sleepy. I'll take her over next Saturday". She looked at me and said, "please. Just do it," and out of sheer stubbornness or maybe either fear, I said, "No, just take me home." It was just a few days later that I woke up, got dressed for work, and was about to head out the door when I got a call from DJ. He had called to tell me that Will had overdosed and died.

Those words landed on me like my heart was being ripped out of my chest. I had to catch myself from falling. I waited for DJ to tell me he was joking, but that never came, nor did the opportunity for me to connect with Will again. Neither did the opportunity for him to meet Alayah. This was another major blow mentally. I felt that if I had been a better friend or the brother that I claimed to be, maybe he wouldn't have overdosed. Maybe he just needed someone to talk to.

I still take that loss just as hard as the loss of my mom because I feel like I could have done something about his addiction.

I apologized to Will's mom for not being there for him. She'd been a second mother to me. She'd sacrificed for me. There were things that she had done for me that I will never be able to repay, and yet I wasn't a friend to her son when he was in a low place. I had sunk to an unfamiliar place. There was no joy in my heart, no joy in my spirit. As time passed, I realized that not only was I mourning my friend, but I was still mourning the loss of my mother. Though I loved them both, I mourned for them in different ways. I missed my mom. She and I couldn't have had a better relationship. We were best friends. There was not another word of adoration that could have been spoken. She knew my heart. I knew hers. And then there was Will. I wished things had been done differently. I wish we would have had a few more conversations. I wish I would've extended myself. I had *regrets.*

There are probably things in your life that you regret, too. They're probably things that you wish you would have done differently in your relationships and in your life. Perhaps there are different decisions you wish you would've made. For me, regret is one of the heaviest weights you can ever carry. It's like driving your car in reverse. You'll never get to where you're supposed to be. That pain will always be with you. You cannot avoid it. I spent years beating myself up about Will. If I'm being honest, I still haven't fully recovered, but I learned something.

I learned that there's one way to beat regret, and that is by **treating each moment as if it may be your last.** Are you living every single day as if it were your last? This page could be the last page you read. That last text conversation could be the last text that you send. I don't say these things to scare you. I say these things to inspire you to live in the moment, to live in the now. Don't let another moment pass that doesn't feel magnificent. God has ordained each and every moment to be intentional. You don't have to live with regret. You don't have to live in reverse. Start maximizing your moments by being present and living in the now.

There are things that I wish I would have done differently as it pertains to my friendship with Will. I missed my moment because I didn't recognize the magnitude of it all, but I've overcome the burden of guilt. I understand that there are a lot of men and women like my best friend, Will, who are struggling with substance abuse, not because they're bad people, but because they're trying to deal with something. I realize that I get opportunities on a daily basis to speak into their lives, to encourage them, to remind them that they are sons and daughters of God, that they have something so much more on the inside of them. And if not anything else, they at least have one person in their corner. And that's me. *Are you living your life on purpose, or are you living your life in reverse?* Let go of it today. Live freely. Realize that today could be your last day, so make it your best.

*If you or someone you know is struggling with substance abuse, please contact
1-800-662-4357(HELP)

In memory of William Arrowood. Your memory lives with me every single day. Thanks for a friendship that will never be matched. I love you bro.

Chapter Nine

Apple Picker

I can remember it like it was yesterday, one of the rare moments I got a chance to go to work with my father. At the time, I was in elementary school and we had only been on spring break from school for about two days. It was an unusually chilly March morning, and I was in the van at 5:00 AM on the way to work with my father and his friends. My dad had worked with his friends (a few Jamaicans and a couple of Mexican guys) for a long time. I think it was their backgrounds of humble beginnings and the journey to the United States that formed the bond. I can remember the loud conversations and if a person wasn't used to people speaking with such heavy accents, they probably

167

wouldn't have understood much of what was being said.

My dad, Syrrant Lynch, was born in Port Antonio, Jamaica, to a father who was a butcher and a mother who was a homemaker. My dad would sometimes talk about his childhood. He'd talk about those long, hot days in Jamaica, playing on a beach and in the Hills. I would vividly try to picture my dad with his brothers and sisters living in one of the most beautiful places in the world. Though the scenery and and Jamacian backdrop is beautiful, my father's life was far from perfect. His dad died at a very young age. My father was only eleven at the time and he was responsible for helping his mother take care of his other siblings. That's a lot of responsibility for anyone, but especially a boy, a boy who was supposed to be in school, a boy who was just supposed to be having fun. Now, the responsibility was on him to lead the household, to be a disciplinarian as well as the person who led by example to help his mother every way possible.

Roughly seven years later, my father was granted a visa to come do migrant work here in the United States. Migrant work is usually seasonal as workers find themselves coming in from other countries to do this very vigorous, difficult, and sometimes strenuous work on a seasonal basis. The workers tend to find themselves on farms and orchards. My father, along with his friends, found themselves working in apple and peach orchards.

I recall hearing other kids talk about the relationships they had with their fathers. They'd talk about their fathers' professions. I was always embarrassed to say what my father did for a living. I wanted to say things like, "My father is a doctor or a policeman" or "my father owns a business", but those who knew me knew that my father was a migrant worker, so in elementary school they'd say "Sean's dad is an apple picker". I now know that term is derogatory.

My dad took a great deal of pride in his profession. That day in the van I looked at my father. He wasn't just happy, he was proud of what he did and how far he had come. He realized the opportunity he had to make a living and to help take care of those he loved.

As we arrived at the orchard, we wouldn't pick any apples as I thought we would be doing; we were going to the orchard to do something far different. My father explained to me that during early spring there are no apples on a tree, but in order for the apples to appear in early or late summer, the trees must be trimmed. Jamaicans say "trim da tree dem", in other words, they were pruning. Pruning is a process of cutting away dead or overgrown branches to increase fruitfulness and growth. Doesn't that sound like something we should do in our lives? Shouldn't we carefully examine the things that aren't conducive to our growth and simply trim or cut them out? Why is it so hard to do that? Why is it so hard to identify the things that bring stress, hurt, anxiety, and pain and remove them?

The relationship I had with my father as a kid was complicated. It's not that I didn't know him. He was in my life; however, our relationship wasn't as deep or intimate as it should have or could have been. There are so many different factors that contributed to my perception of my father as I was growing up. I had to see past what I was seeing. I had to go deeper. I had to remove or prune the things that were going to keep me from seeing him in a more positive light. I spent a lot of my youth not feeling as though he loved or cared for me. The relationship between him and my mother was also an unusual one. There was a pretty significant age difference between the two of them, so a lot of their ideologies and even social practices were different, not to mention the cultural differences. My dad would sometimes come to our apartment with my sister, Kayla (she's about 8 months younger than me). We would all eat dinner, spend some time together and they'd eventually leave. There was always a sense of bitterness or resentment in my spirit.

There was just another level of knowing that I wanted, that I needed, that I longed for, small things that people with fathers take for granted. I knew him, but I didn't *really* know him. Things like random roughhousing or banter or just taking a long ride in their car, just the two of us getting to know each other and bonding. Even knowing my father's favorite song or color could have altered the way I felt about him. Between the ages of nine and twelve, I played in countless basketball games. I wanted nothing more than for my father to be at them. I recognize now in hindsight that there were reasons he didn't come, that there were certain preferences, certain things that he had going on, but as a young boy, I didn't understand. I decided the reason he didn't show up was because he did not love me. I was hurt. There was pain that would take a long time for me to get over or even acknowledge.

The removal of old thoughts was dependent upon my new way of looking at things. I had to cut back some thoughts and resentment that kept me from getting to know him. I had to tear down those walls that I had built up. Those perceptions I had about my father changed significantly the older I got. I began to look past the hurt and started to appreciate the person, the man, the father that he was.

As a little boy, that day on the orchard, I not only saw the pride that he had, I saw how hard he worked. I saw that every tree he trimmed was almost as if it was the first. With each tree, he paid incredible attention to detail. He didn't leave any piece of bark that wasn't supposed to be present. His work ethic and attention to detail on everything he did was unmatched. I didn't realize that then, but the older I got, I realized that those are qualities that allow you to stand out above the rest. My father didn't make it to school past the sixth grade, yet he was willing and able to help others and take care of his family because of his work ethic.

They say sometimes it takes dark moments to appreciate the light. As much as I love my mother, I realized she played a part in my not having a relationship with my father as a kid. Though I don't harbor any negative feelings about my mother because I love her and I'm biased; I do however realize that if she had done some things differently my father and I would've had a better relationship.

It was actually shortly after my mother's death that my father and I began to bond. I began reaching out directly to my dad for advice and support. I began to see him in a new light, we were bonding in a way we never had before. I just hate that it took twenty-one years for me to get to know him on such a personal level. As I mentioned, the darkness of my mother's passing, led to deeper depths in my relationship with my father.

My father would say things like, "Accept the things you cannot change" or he'd say, "what a person says and does are two different things". I came to appreciate my father's unparalleled wisdom. He earned the nickname Wizard from his friends for his unmatched wisdom. As I matured, his wisdom became soothing because no matter the situation or what I was going through, I knew without a shadow of a doubt, he would lend a fresh perspective and point me toward the right solution.

Although in my youth, my father and I never had a 'bonding' activity, we certainly formed one over the past few years. One bonding activity came in the form of raking and bagging leaves in my yard. Though I don't like manual labor at all, I came to look forward to spending time in the yard with my dad. Much like those car rides I wish we had gone on as a kid, the process of us raking leaves allowed us so many hours just to talk and get to know each other. I never had time to stop to take breaks though. My job was only to hold the bag of leaves while my father would stuff the bag. I can say that I got to know my dad on such a deep level doing something as tedious as raking leaves. Now that I think about it, there's so much irony in that. As trees transition from one season to the other, they lose their leaves. I was much like those very trees. I had to lose the leaves of an old season in order to embrace the relationship with my father in a new season.

Do you know of a person who has the ability to fill up a room with their presence alone? Just being honest, I don't know many, but my father is one of those people. His presence is one of both peace and power. He has the ability to calm a person's spirit while also encouraging them to be bold in the face of what they're dealing with, *peace* and *power*.

It was a random April night in 2018 and I had just so happened to be at my father's house, dropping something off. At that time in my life, I was in the middle of making a pretty big decision as it pertained to my career. I really had no peace, just stress and anxiety. Upon leaving my father's house that night, I left empowered to enter the next season of my life with complete peace and clarity. To take it a step further, for the first time, we talked about the relationship we had when I was a kid. Though it was one of the most vulnerable conversations my father and I ever had, it was definitely the best to date.

I was in the yard raking leaves, alone, when my phone rang. It was my brother-in- law, Travis. I could hear fear and panic in his voice, he said, "You need to get to your dad's house now". I threw down the rake and ran inside. My heart was pounding. So many thoughts were going through my head. It was Cinco de Mayo, 2018. Michelle and I were supposed to be going out for Mexican food, now I was in my car and speeding through town. It felt as though the faster I tried to drive, the slower I'd move. As my car's four way flashers blinked, I ran red lights and stop signs. I pulled into my dad's development to find countless police cars and fire trucks, though nothing was on fire. My heart dropped as I saw my sister Kayla, Travis, and my nephews, outside my father's house. I turned to run in, only to be stopped by a firefighter.

Our father was getting older. As I mentioned earlier, he was quite a bit older than my mother. He had entered what appeared to be the early stages of dementia. We would often tell him to make sure he did not turn on the car while it was in the garage or to make sure he turned the stove off. My sister, Kalya and I were at ease because our older half sister, Huverlyn, was visiting from Jamaica. She had been staying with dad to both connect with and look after him for a little while.

All we could do was wait. It was the most helpless and vulnerable I'd ever felt. Both my father and older sister were in the house and we had no idea if they were dead or alive. As I stood in the road in front of the house trying to grasp what was going on, I saw one of the firefighters make his way out of the house towards me, I decided to meet him halfway. As we met in the front yard, it had started to rain. He placed his hand on my shoulder and told me the news that both my father and half sister had passed away as a result of carbon monoxide poisoning. It was what I had suspected. The night prior, my father went into the garage, started the car, returned upstairs and forgot to go back down to turn the vehicle off.

It was one of the worst pieces of information I'd ever received-- to lose a father and a sister in that fashion on the same day was traumatic. It was our worst nightmare. As I write this, I don't know that I've fully dealt with their losses and the way they passed. Of all things, carbon monoxide. There's not a lot of things more dangerous than carbon monoxide. It's odorless and tasteless. You don't see it coming; you don't even smell it coming. It just comes and eliminates.

Rousawn M. Dozier

It reminds me of the things in life that sometimes hinder us and set us back. It's not the big things that we see. It's not those big decisions that we make. It's the small decisions, the itty bitty ones that aren't conducive to our growth on a daily basis. And we look back after a traumatic or life-defining moment, and we try to determine how we got there. *It was the small things, the little things that we didn't see.*

I think about the carbon monoxide and how it crept up on my father, one of the strongest men I've ever met. We mourned. We were sad, but it's always about the perspective you take. Perspective is so important, it drives performance. I remember my father saying, "accept the things you cannot change". I can't change the fact that he's not here. So, I accept it, and by accepting it, it gives me peace. I got to know him on an intimate level and ultimately he helped me become a better man; that gives me joy. I'm grateful that he was able to meet and get to know two of my three children.

I can still hear the sound of the tree clippers trimming away dead leaves. And I think to myself, *What do I need to trim today? What do I need to cut out of my life? What do I need to trim on my perspective so that I can see people in a new way, so that I can see myself in a new way?*

I guess I could have titled this chapter "Lessons from My Father," but I thought I'd honor him by giving it the title, "Apple Picker". Although some may see it as a derogatory term, my father was proud of what he did. As a man, I recognize that no matter what his title was, it couldn't have held or explained his greatness and that an apple picker did more to impact his family, friends, and people, in his community than a lot of doctors or lawyers.

Dad, until we meet again, thank you for loving and getting to know me. Thank you for the wisdom you left me with. I wish we could have gotten to know each other better, but guess what? I'm going to accept the things I cannot change and embrace those in which I can.

Chapter Ten

Becoming the Architect

From the time I was a kid, I always had an appreciation for buildings. I would and still do spend countless hours admiring architecture from around the world -- both new age and ancient. When admiring incredible structures, I think about the many men and women who gave so much of their time and lives to ensure the building or structure was completed with excellence. The problem with going straight to the building is that I miss a very important part -- a critical part -- the *design* of it. Yes, taking a dream and making a clear and concise plan as to how it will be built -- this is *architecture*. It's the very careful and/or complex process of designing something.

184

I believe, without a shadow of a doubt, that we -- yes, you and I--are the architects of our minds and lives. I am fully confident that with the right effort we can design the lives we want for ourselves. Think back to the twins I mentioned in the introduction. Both were exposed to harsh realities as children through adulthood. Essentially, both experienced trauma and were made to deal with post-traumatic trauma. However, the two each created completely different versions of their futures. Why was one twin successful, having experienced an emotionally and physically painful childhood, while the other one essentially never escaped it? I believe the answer is: one purposefully and decisively designed the future he wanted, and the other didn't. One became the architect.

You see, *your mind is like a radio station and the universe is like waves*. Those who can remember having to listen to the radio while in the car will also

remember trying to set the tuner on a station so that

the sound could come through clearly. *Your mind has

the power to adjust the signal you receive. In other

words, you can always change the station.* You can

attract and design the future you desire. At this point,

you're probably saying to yourself, "How?" You

become the architect of your future by doing three

things in particular:

1. Dream it!

It's been said, "*It takes the same amount of energy to

dream big as it does to dream small.*" Since we were

kids, we've all had dreams of doing great things. At

some point, something or someone convinced us that

our dreams were too big. I'm challenging you to

dream big again. The world needs what you have

inside of you. Communities need your brilliance. Your

children need your example. Architects begin not with

their pen on the paper, but rather their heads in the clouds. The buildings that I enjoy looking at are just manifestations of the visions God placed in the minds and hearts of the architects. Never under any circumstance downplay your dreams. They may seem too big for some, but if it came to you, it can also come from you.

I was once in a place where I thought my dreams were limited to the experiences I had as a kid and young man. That is so far from the truth. I challenge you to get out of your past and begin dreaming with your great great grandchildren in mind.

2. Design it!

Once the architect gets the vision, he or she sits down and designs what they see in their minds. They spend time meticulously laying out each and every measurement and angle. There is no detail too small.

This is where the architect takes full control and designs their future. This is why it's important that you don't wish to go back and start over after experiencing hardships. The power comes when your perspective turns your losses into lessons. **Your life lessons are your honorary PhD** and you have the power to leverage them to your benefit rather than allowing them to be your detriment. Your past, while certain areas may be painful, can be the best tool for you to use to move forward.

Every single story I shared with you helped shape me. Yes, some of those experiences hurt. In all honesty, I didn't know how I'd manage to get through some of them. I now know that I have the power to extract the gold from the mines of darkness.

3. Do it!

A mentor of mine once said, "So many people's destinies are tied to your obedience." I absolutely love that and in this case I'll say, "So many people's destinies are tied to you DOING what you're supposed to do." Sadly, a lot of gifted and talented people don't live up to their potential, not because they skipped dreaming and designing, but because they fail to take action! *Action creates separation;* separation from who you were and builds a bridge to who God has created you to be. The "do it" phase is also where you gain confidence. You're vulnerable in this phase. It's the phase where you put yourself "out there," but guess what? There's no better place to be. The only way to grow is to be stretched, and the only way to be stretched is to do something that makes you uncomfortable. The cool thing about being stretched is that like a rubberband, you can never go back to the size you were before the stretching.

Can I Just Start Over?!

There you have it. That's how you become the architect of your life. That's how I became the architect of mine. I stopped running from my past, and I embraced it. The good parts, the bad parts and certainly the ugly ones. So, the next time you ask yourself, Can I Just Start Over?! you'll know that the power is not in starting over...it's in starting now.

Rousawn M. Dozier

About the Author

Rousawn has been described as charismatic, humorous, inspirational and communicative. However, if you're familiar with his story, you'd probably refer to him as an overcomer. Raised in a government assisted single-parent household, Rousawn was exposed to poverty and violence in his youth. Every single day posed challenges and adversity; adversity that pushed Rousawn to the limit. Refusing to allow hardships to overcome him, Rousawn changed his perspective and began viewing his obstacles as opportunities to grow his mind, character and will power.

Today, Rousawn is a keynote speaker, consultant and mindset architect, a nickname he earned from his coaching clients. As a master storyteller, Rousawn Dozier wows audiences with passion, humor, and his dynamic approach on living a life of purpose. Individuals, teams and corporations have been impacted by his real, relational and transparent messages on how to be the architect of their lives. He trains and equips audiences to overcome fixed mindsets, limiting beliefs and fear by providing simple and applicable action steps.

Rousawn is the founder of Rousawn Dozier & Associates and the Dozier Legacy Foundation. In addition to being a certified coach and speaker, Rousawn holds a Master of Business Administration (MBA). He resides in the eastern Panhandle of West Virginia with his wife Michelle, two daughters, Alayah and Abrie, and his son, Ari.

Connect with the Author

Website: www.RousawnDozier.com

Facebook: @RouawnMDozier

Instagram: @RousawnDozier

LinkedIn: @RousawnDozier

Twitter: @RousawnDozier

Can you do me a favor?

Thank you for taking the time to read this book. It truly means the world to me. I'm forever grateful!

Would you mind taking 60 seconds to review this book on Amazon?

Reviews are the best way for independent authors like myself, to get noticed, sell more books, and spread positive messages to as many people as possible. More importantly, *a portion of proceeds from each book sold will go towards sending individuals to a therapy session.*

Made in United States
North Haven, CT
16 July 2024

54854029R00118